Stephen K. De Silva

PROSPEROUS HOME

A Basic Guide to
Budgeting and Money Management

BOOK ONE

Prosperous Home

A Basic Guide to Budgeting and Money Management

Stephen K. De Silva

ISBN: 978-0-9968853-2-4

Written by Stephen K. De Silva
Book Cover Design: Joshua Read
Publishing: De Silva Ministries
Book Formatting: Red Dove Publishing
Website: Reddovedesign.com
Printed in the United States of America.
First printing, 2016

ACKNOWLEDGEMENTS

This book is dedicated to my parents, Beth and Earl, for a debt I cannot repay.

TABLE OF CONTENTS

INTRODUCTION

This administration today, here and now, declares unconditional war on poverty in America. I urge this Congress and all Americans to join with me in that effort.

President Lyndon B. Johnson, January 8, 1964

Americans have waged a war on poverty for over fifty years. In April 2012, the National Health Statistics Report[1] published observations on our progress. From that report, they observed that the average child-bearing age of a college-degreed woman is 30.1 years, bearing an average of 1.1 children. In comparison, the average female without a high school diploma or GED of 15-18 years will bear an average of 2.5 children. Over 90 years, the generational multiple for the educated woman in the middle class over three generations totals 3.3 children. Meanwhile, the uneducated woman in poverty will see five generations in that same timespan, and bear a total of 48.6 children. This is a ratio of 15:1. Simply put, those born into poverty in our nation are exponentially more than those born into relative wealth. And the birth rate is only one factor contributing to the widening divide between rich and poor in the West.

1 *Martinez Ph.D.; Daniels, Ph.D.; Chandra, Ph.D., Fertility of Men and Women Aged 15–44 Years in the United States: National Survey of Family Growth, 2006–2010. (PHS) 2012-1250. Division of Vital Statistics; No. 51. (Hyattsville, MD: National Center for Health Statistics. April 12, 2012), 29.*

In January 2014, the Council of Economic Advisors published a report on fifty years of progress.[2] Here is one quote from that official publication:

> *While the United States is often seen as the land of economic opportunity, only about half of low-income Americans make it out of the lowest income distribution quintile over a 20-year period. About 40 percent of the differences in parents' income are reflected in children's income as they become adults, pointing to strong, lingering effects from growing up in poverty.*

I applaud the foresight and determination of President Johnson and the countless men and women who have labored tirelessly over the past half-century in this war against poverty. However, poverty will not be defeated using politics and science alone. This is because poverty, in its essence, is a spiritual battle.

I consider government efforts to be appropriate but incomplete. They have rightly identified the chronic and persistent social disease of poverty. They have diligently approved programs and studies for ending this unacceptable condition that afflicts American homes and lives. But poverty is a spiritual matter and its defeat will require help from God through His earthly institution, the Church. This curriculum represents precisely that help. Prosperous Home uses spiritual tools to shatter incorrect ideas and patterns to solve the problem of poverty one household at a time. These tools, combined with the efforts of governments and well-intentioned agencies, can finally win the war on poverty. Prosperous Home is a practical system for teaching the mechanics of money. Using language that is simple yet powerful, the reader can develop and manage their own Prosperous Home.

I hope to see all homes healed and transformed, not merely American homes. Prosperous Home, therefore, is designed to add value regardless of your nation of residence. I have seen these tools traverse cultures, ages, and economic levels. I observe it benefiting families, businesses, churches, and governments. I am confident that the curriculum is effective, having taught these keys to people like you in many parts of the world.

So let it do the same for you. Gain your foothold in the war against poverty. Begin your personal climb toward financial strength. As God prospers you, choose to partner and cooperate with His design, and see your family become a Prosperous Home.

---

2 *The War on Poverty 50 Years Later: A Progress Report.*

HOW TO USE THIS MANUAL

This manual is designed to bring health and life to your home finances by training you in three areas:

I. First, I will address how your heart and mindsets play a crucial role in the success of your finances. Money is a spiritual power and you must recognize it as such. (To go deeper into the spiritual aspects of money and how to align your heart and mind with Heaven's economy, you will need to get my Prosperous Soul material.)
II. Second, I will introduce you to the practical tools to create a healthy financial home.
III. Finally, I will provide insights that elevate your idea of wealth, and help you begin to build a plan that will create a long-lasting impact on your personal financial goals.

There are a number of ways to use this manual. You can just read through it and learn the material. This will provide some benefit in changing your relationship to money. However, at the end of each chapter, there are activities and questions to help you put the concepts and strategies into practice. If you do nothing else, doing the homework in each chapter will at least give you the basic framework for building a Prosperous Home. However, the best way to use this manual is to go through it with a group using the Prosperous Home Leader's Guide and the Prosperous Home Video Curriculum. You can get everything you need to lead or start a Prosperous Home Group by getting the Prosperous Home Curriculum Kit. There are online tools you can use as well.

At the end of each chapter you will find these different categories to enrich your experience:

HOMEWORK	This section is designed to reinforce the main lessons for a Prosperous Home. These activities and worksheets build the skeletal structure to your home finances and give you the tools necessary to think like a prosperous soul. (If you need extra copies of the worksheets, you can find them in the back of the book.)
VIDEO	This section shows you which videos correlate with each chapter. If there are handouts or worksheets that accompany the chapter, this section will also point you to the appropriate video tutorial to help in filling out the worksheets.
GOING DEEPER	These questions are designed to help you think more deeply, master the material, and make it more personal.
FURTHER STUDY	This section is for heavy thinkers and researchers. These books, messages, and references are where the ideas discussed in the chapter are developed further. Going through these resources will help you master this material.
PRAYER	It can be easy to leave God out of the conversation when it comes to your finances. This section has dictated prayers to help you engage with God and His heart for your finances.
PROPHETIC ACTS	This section suggests prophetic acts and declarations to help activate your faith to see God's promises fulfilled for your finances. These are small items that you can do daily. You will see a huge impact as you engage your faith with God's heart.

CHAPTER 01

POWER TO EXAGGERATE

Money is a spiritual power and spiritual power will always exaggerate whatever lies hidden in a person's heart. Unfortunately, many people have suffered under the exaggerating power of money by failing to understand this one fact.

Consider these observations about money. First, it is inanimate and can do nothing by its own initiative. Money has no mind, no opinion, and no agenda. Money is neither good nor evil, but perfectly amoral as an object. Money functions like a tool. As it is used, we discover not the character of the tool, but the heart of its possessor.

Imagine a hammer lying on the ground. Alone, it is powerless and can only wait to be chosen. Along comes someone who discovers the hammer. This person may use it for good by building and creating, or for evil by breaking and harming. In either case, the hammer's only power is in revealing the heart of its possessor. This is the case with any tool, but with money, the effect is many times more exaggerated. Money makes hidden things bigger.

God engineered money this way in order to "show and tell" a person's heart. When God sees something pleasing, He gives rewards with the hope of producing more good. Of course, God rewards with many things besides money, but money is uniquely suited for exaggerating hidden things.

And without faith it is impossible to please Him, for he who comes to God must believe that He is and that He is a rewarder of those who seek Him.

Hebrews 11:6 NASB

Money is a blessing, and God uses money to bless His children. We know God wouldn't give us a stone if we ask for bread. Therefore, we can see that money is good, fun, just, and something powerful we get to carry with wisdom and care.

God said to Solomon, "Because you had this in mind, and did not ask for riches, wealth or honor, or the life of those who hate you, nor have you even asked for long life, but you have asked for yourself wisdom and knowledge that you may rule My people over whom I have made you king, wisdom and knowledge have been granted to you. And I will give you riches and wealth and honor, such as none of the kings who were before you has possessed nor those who will come after you."

2 Chronicles 1:11-12 NASB

It is the blessing of the LORD that makes rich, And He adds no sorrow to it.

Proverbs 10:22 NASB

Or what man is there among you who, when his son asks for a loaf, will give him a stone? Or if he asks for a fish, he will not give him a snake, will he? If you then, being evil, know how to give good gifts to your children, how much more will your Father who is in heaven give what is good to those who ask Him!

Matthew 7:9-11 NASB

SPIRIT MEANS ATTITUDE

When I say money is a spiritual power, it is important to communicate clearly and accurately, according to the Bible. The word "spirit" is similar for both Old Testament (Hebrew: rûach) and New Testament (Greek: pneuma). Literally, it means breath or wind. But figuratively, spirit can refer to humanity, super-humanity (angels and demons), or divinity (God).

HUMAN	SUPER-HUMAN	DIVINE
Attitudes and mindsets	Angels and demons	God and Holy Spirit
Genesis 45:27	1 Samuel 16:14	Genesis 1:2
Colossians 2:5	Matthew 12:43	John 4:24

When resolving spiritual issues surrounding money, it is important to understand that I am referring to attitudes and mindsets, not demons. Money exaggerates what is inside ourselves, and by inside, I mean attitudes and mindsets we hold to be true about ourselves, others, and God. Sometimes we hold to things that are biblically true, and other times we hold to things that are biblically untrue. For example, the idea "I am significant" is biblically true; the idea "I am worthless" is biblically untrue.

I can and have dealt with demons, but I understand they are not the real issue. In the same way that flies are attracted to stinky things, demons are attracted the destructive behaviors that money will exaggerate when a person holds to beliefs that are unbiblical (untrue and stinky). Demons simply come along to exploit the opportunity, and all that needs to be done to deal with them is to cast them out. The real spiritual issue that must be addressed is the unbiblical beliefs. This is the unique advantage of Prosperous Home; it enables a person to change his or her attitudes and mindsets and get past his or her unbiblical spiritual obstacles.

Therefore if you have been raised up with Christ, keep seeking the things above, where Christ is, seated at the right hand of God. Set your mind on the things above, not on the things that are on earth. For you have died and your life is hidden with Christ in God. When Christ, who is our life, is revealed, then you also will be revealed with Him in glory.

Colossians 3:1-4 NASB

POVERTY AND MAMMON

Money is not demonic, but demons do exploit the human attitudes and mindsets (spirits) we call poverty and mammon. Both spirits represent lies that must be displaced using biblical truth. If these spirits were demons, Christians would simply cast them out according to Jesus' own words:

"And as you go, preach, saying, 'The kingdom of heaven is at hand.' Heal the sick, raise the dead, cleanse the lepers, cast out demons. Freely you received, freely give."

Matthew 10:7-8 NASB

Poverty spirits and mammon spirits are resilient because we cannot cast out an attitude or mindset. Instead, these must be displaced. Because money is a spiritual power, the devil seeks to exploit its power at every opportunity. To confuse and trap people, the devil exploits powerful things using pairs of extremes. He attempts to draw us into one extreme by distracting us with our extra dislike of the other. Around money, the paired extremes are the spirits of poverty and mammon.[3]

An efficient biblical translation of the phrase "poverty spirit" would be a "beggary attitude." To a contemporary mind, these two words best capture the biblical implication and application of what is meant when someone refers to a "poverty spirit" or having a poverty "mindset."

3 *For more information and exercises on overcoming the spirits of poverty and mammon, see my manual entitled Prosperous Soul—Foundations at www.prosperoussoul.com/store.*

Poverty thinking holds a person back and will strategically condemn to perpetuate defeat. It is a victim mindset that drains away hope, courage, and momentum. Partnering with a poverty mindset depresses and oppresses everyone under its influence, and is ultimately exacerbated by the demonic because it fundamentally partners with a lie.

A mammon spirit is also an attitude and not a demon. Jesus spoke clearly against this as a terrible and unacceptable spirit. An efficient biblical translation of mammon spirit would be "money deified," which happens when someone worships money to gain the benefits of its power. Mammon is an embezzling spirit that trades influence for worship. Mammon pushes you beyond your boundaries, addicting and intoxicating while fueling entitlement and greed.

Mammon demonstrates the opposite characteristics of a poverty spirit, just as a mirror reverses a reflection. Below is a brief comparison of these two spirits. Consider the outside columns as opposites on a teeter-totter and the center column as the fulcrum. The devil cares little about which opposing attitude we wrestle with, only that we fixate on one in an effort to avoid the other, thereby missing the biblical center entirely. The middle column represents this center, where our redeemed condition as God's sons and daughters bring us through to hope and purpose. I've chosen the words carefully. Study them thoughtfully and ask Holy Spirit if there is any evidence of these mindsets presently in your life.

POVERTY SPIRIT	PROSPEROUS SOUL	MAMMON SPIRIT
Victim	Hero	Villain
Lack	Abundance	Excess
Prey	Protector	Predatory
Suspicious	Gracious	Condemning
Hoarding	Stewarding	Greedy
Disqualified	Acceptance	Entitlement

Poverty and mammon are spiritual influences that we all must learn to resist. Each of these spirits has its own attraction that pulls upon our internal wounds and beliefs like magnets. Each features a host of pitfalls, both literal and spiritual, that are disastrous to wealth. Some believers perceive these influences to be normal parts of everyday life—they have allowed these spirits to become familiar—and unintentionally invite their destructive effects into their lives. Other believers overcompensate in their avoidance of one spirit, putting themselves at risk of falling under the influence of the other. We must continually consult the Holy Spirit for guidance and allow Him to train our vision upon our ultimate goal—Jesus, the One who has gone before us as our perfect model of stewardship and the embodiment of a prosperous soul.

A PROSPEROUS SOUL

None of us can gain real victory over the spiritual power of money without mastering our own heart. We receive this through the redeeming and restoring work of the Holy Spirit, which is available to anyone who asks. If you have confessed Christ as Savior and Lord, you can expect the miracle of a prosperous soul. If you have not given yourself to Christ, ask a follower of Jesus how to become a Christian. It will be the best decision of your life and your eternity. Everyone who partners with money will need to take this important step in order to have real mastery over money.

A born-again believer can develop a prosperous soul because of the redemption provided by Jesus on the cross. A prosperous soul is simply a soul that has surrendered its former unbiblical beliefs in exchange for biblical truth. Lies and wounds are given away and truth is exchanged in the person's soul.

The Holy Spirit alone gives us the ability to exchange lies for truth, and you cannot fake this fact. Where poverty and mammon target possessions and circumstances, they also work to diminish our soul's capacity for carrying wealth. A prosperous soul is a soul aimed at God-given purpose, undeterred in accomplishing its destiny with God and money.

> *Beloved, I pray that in all respects you may prosper and be in good health, just as your soul prospers.*
>
> *3 John 1:2 NASB*

LESSONS
CHAPTER ONE

HOMEWORK

Take the Prosperous Soul Quiz online at www.prosperoussoul.com/quiz.

VIDEO

Watch video #1 entitled, "Spiritual Power of Money," on your DVD or online curriculum.

GOING DEEPER

In what way is money a spiritual power?

How have you noticed mindsets affecting money?

How does money exaggerate the heart?

What do you think the Bible means in 3 John 1:2?

Describe poverty and mammon in your own words.

What is the purpose of money?

What is God's heart for money?

What are your fears with money? Refer to the *Curious List of Lies* at pages 218-220.

Look back at the Poverty/Prosperous Soul/Mammon chart. Do you find yourself on that chart? Are there any areas of improvement?

FURTHER STUDY

Read Stephen's book, Money and the Prosperous Soul.

Sign up for Stephen's Prosperous Soul course.

Read or memorize these verses: Psalms 119:14, Philippians 4:19, 1 Timothy 6:17.

PRAYER

Father God, thank You for the invitation to become a prosperous soul. I ask You to show me where I need to grow. Reveal every mindset that hinders my soul from prospering according to the Bible. Give me courage in the journey to passionately and powerfully pursue a healthy financial home for my family.

PROPHETIC ACT

Declare this over your life this week: "I AM A PROSPEROUS SOUL!"

NOTES

CHAPTER 02

A REASON FOR WHY

Most financial courses major on how money should be managed according to the instructor's beliefs. They concentrate on pragmatic diagrams and spreadsheets that generalize skills and rules surrounding money. This impersonal model pursues financial success in a vacuum of purpose, quite like traveling far by watching your feet—you eventually get somewhere, but the destination is purely accidental. The Prosperous Home approach is different. In this manual, we identify the reason why we have money and what it means to steward according to that reason. This approach brings context to the pragmatic and orients us to steward our money from a higher perspective than day-to-day needs. God is the Giver of purpose, creating a genuine environment for experiencing financial health. Mastery of budgeting and investing can flow from an authentic expression of our financial why.

Measuring success in a Prosperous Home focuses on fulfillment of purpose rather than the demonstration of accuracy with diagrams and spreadsheets. It is said that money is the perfect slave. If that is true, then money is perfectly designed to serve you in your God-given purpose. My favorite definition for success, which I've taken from Viktor E. Frankl's book, Man's Search for Meaning, follows beautifully here. Frankl says that success cannot be pursued; it must ensue, and it only does so as the unintended side effect of one's personal dedication to a cause greater than oneself, or as the byproduct of one's surrender to a person other than oneself. Success will follow you precisely because you have forgotten to think of it.[4]

4 *Viktor Frankl, Man's Search for Meaning, (New York, NY: Pocket Books, 1985), 17.*

People who master their money are simply people who use money to accomplish their purpose. For the Christian, purpose is much deeper than dogged persistence and obedience to spreadsheets. Mastery of money is satisfying for the Christian because it demonstrates our co-laboring with God to accomplish the meaning of our lives. God is loving and engaged with us. He is a Father, almighty and aware. Our God is love, and our ability to hear, obey, and work together will attract the world to Christ. This is what I call an evangelism of jealousy. It is what a queen from antiquity saw in a staircase[5] and what the apostle Paul foreshadowed as a mystery.[6]

Traditional home budgeting materials focus on earning and spending, which is income-statement-oriented. Better materials expand that focus to include debt and savings, which is still incomplete. We will improve on all these efforts by understanding purpose, then building net worth accordingly, allowing for a true measure of financial success. Before we go any further, let's explore my important tool called The Purpose Train.[7]

PURPOSE TRAIN

Money is a spiritual power, and power will always exaggerate whatever is hidden in your heart.[8]

The Purpose Train is a simple way to articulate your purpose as it relates to money. Separate materials on the tool are available if you choose to go deeper in this lesson. For now, we will use a simplified version to articulate your Prosperous Home purpose.

God designed you with a purpose in mind, so money is just one of many tools available to accomplish that purpose. Purpose answers the question, "Why was I born?" Caring, leading, serving, giving—these are each powerful ways of fulfilling your why. Understanding your financial why is a fundamental step. Some of us go, while others send, but neither of these actions are answers to the question, "Why was I born?" Likewise, money is a means and never an end to matters of purpose. Your first assignment will be to clearly articulate your financial why using the Purpose Train tool.

5 *Reference for Queen of Sheba from 2 Chronicles.*
6 *1 Corinthians 4:1.*
7 *For more information, find my titles, Purpose Train Book and Purpose Train Handbook for Organizations.*
8 *Find more on the spiritual aspects of money in my book, Money and the Prosperous Soul.*

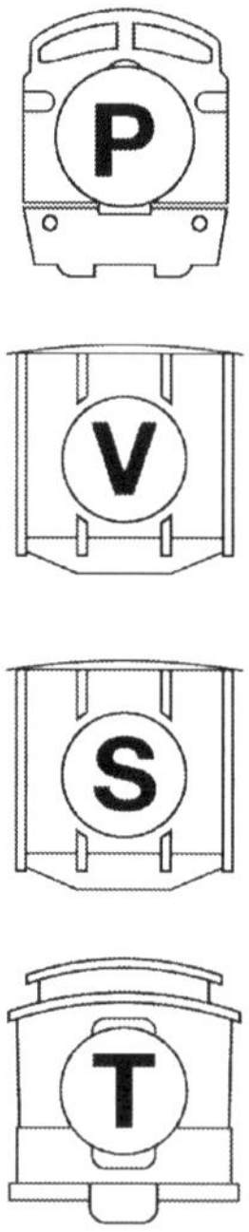

Begin with four boxes drawn vertically, linked by a chain in the manner of a train. Each box represents a different mode of thinking and symbolizes our responsibility to adapt and preside like judges over our many personal choices and decisions.

Purpose answers the question:	"Why was I born?"
Vision answers the question:	"What do I see?"
Strategies answer the question:	"How I get there?"
Tactics answer the daily question:	"Shall I decide yes or no?"

Most of us operate in a Tactical mode, meaning we push the train from behind in reaction to the endless urgencies and demands that assault us daily at a detail level. Since Tactics feel urgent, we spend much of our time like firefighters trying to extinguish the continual fires that spark around us. Living at the Tactical level makes day-to-day life seem like an endless circle of wildfires.

Tactical decisions made well are accidental unless they are led by something higher. Tactics best follow Strategies, which is the next boxcar. Everyone knows that trains move best when pulled. Rather than pushing a Tactical lifestyle, you should pull them from a higher mode of Strategic thinking. A good Strategy will decide most of your Tactical decisions for you.

Strategies are effective at pulling Tactics behind them, but both Tactics and Strategies are similar in this way: they are better pulled than pushed. Strategy follows something higher, which is Vision—the next boxcar. Making Strategic decisions without clear Vision is again like pushing your Purpose Train from behind.

However, while thinking from Vision mode can take you further and longer than either Strategy or Tactics, it too will eventually derail with exhaustion and frustration. A derail at the Tactical level is called a mistake. A derail at the Strategic level is called a case of poor judgment. A derail at the Visionary level is called a mid-life crisis.

SIMPLIFIED EXAMPLE

Let's work with a common example of a Tactical conflict. Imagine a family with limited cash and credit card debt. Should they use that cash to build savings or pay off debt? Both are effective tactics, but they compete with one another, since money can only be directed to one place or the other. This leaves the decision-maker feeling conflicted and confused about choosing the right answer. The Purpose Train will solve this problem by allowing the engine of Purpose to pull the optimal Vision, Strategy, and Tactics. Let's pause our example and first build the family's Purpose Train.

Imagine the family sets aside time to consider prayerfully why the family exists. They first affirm that they exist to care for and support one another. Care and support are things you see, and therefore belong in the Vision box. As they continue to ask themselves about their why, they begin to assemble broad and powerful Purpose words like "save," "worship," and "rescue." They like "save" because it captures their purpose for evangelizing the world. They like "worship" because it captures their purpose of glorifying God in all they say and do. They like "rescue" because it captures their passion for helping the weak and oppressed. These are the highest words they can think of to describe why the family exists.

During a Purpose Training session, I use their chosen words and work at combining them or moving them to lower boxcars. For example, the family decided that "worship" was something they saw (a Vision word) and that "save" and "rescue" were so similar that they should be combined and lowered to the Strategy box. This left the Purpose box empty. However, the exercise reminded the parents of a verse in Proverbs that captured all these ideas in a concise spiritual image. They chose the word "tower" to capture the idea of why the family existed.

The name of the LORD is a strong tower; The righteous runs into it and is safe.

Proverbs 18:10 NASB

This refining process continued down the Purpose Train tool. For the Vision boxcar, they combined and refined what they saw for the family down to one word: "strength." They chose this word because the family sees themselves as a "tower" by living in strength with permanent debt freedom. Strategy follows next. Since chronic credit card balances threaten their Vision, the Strategy is to permanently shatter that cycle; therefore the family chose the Strategic key word shatter. Finally, Tactics trail last, which brought us back to the two competing Tactics—whether to pay off debt or build savings. The Purpose Train illustrates the Tactical conflict by setting the competing Tactics side by side (see illustration). But which Tactic has the priority?

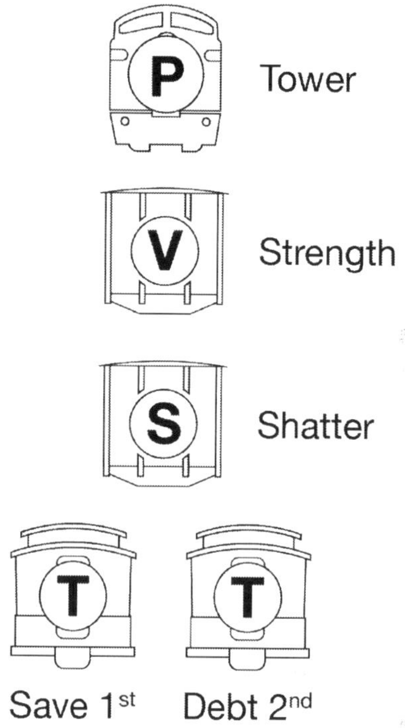

Although the pay-down of debt seems obvious, the Purpose Train alignment identifies a better approach. Reading from the top down, the family will be a "tower of strength that forever shatters the debt cycle." The Vision of forever shattering the debt cycle becomes the deciding factor, placing the payoff of debt second to their glaring need for saving an emergency fund. Debt reduction is important but secondary to an emergency fund; otherwise the family remains vulnerable to unforeseen troubles and risks perpetuating the debt cycle. Without an emergency fund, debt threatens to repeat itself over and over again. For a Prosperous Home, building an adequate emergency fund serves as a bumper against the predictable but unknown emergencies of life. This is how a debt cycle is permanently shattered, enabling a family to rise above debt forever. This is a simplified example of one family's Purpose Train.

What is most powerful about the Purpose Train tool is the process of finding and refining meaningful words from the top down. This is extremely helpful in solving seemingly complex and conflicting Tactical problems in individuals, homes, and organizations. If you want more on this subject, I recommend that you see my other materials on The Purpose Train, or seek individual coaching through my website: www.prosperoussoul.com.

Use the Purpose Train format at the end of this chapter to refine your own Prosperous Home Purpose, Vision, Strategy, and Tactics. Allow time and energy to write, re-write, and refine your words until your best version is captured in the spaces below. This step is vital for defining success in your own Prosperous Home.

LESSONS
CHAPTER TWO

HOMEWORK

Fill out your Purpose Train (on page 34).

VIDEO

Watch video #2 entitled, "A Reason for Why," on your DVD or online curriculum.

GOING DEEPER

How would being motivated by Purpose change your day-to-day life?

Why did you choose the Purpose word you chose?

What Tactics do you need to change or discard because of your Purpose Train?

How can you use the Purpose Train to bring clarity and intentionality to other areas of your life besides finances?

What would living on purpose look and feel like?

What did the Queen of Sheba see in a staircase and what does Paul mean when he talks of mystery?

FURTHER STUDY

Read the story of Solomon (2 Chronicles 9:1-12).

Read Stephen's booklet, The Purpose Train for Organizations.

Listen to Stephen's message, "Shirtless in My Offering."

Read or memorize these verses: 2 Chronicles 9:3-4, 1 Corinthians 4:1.

PRAYER

Father God, thank You for creating me for a purpose. I ask You to bring clarity into what You have created me to do, and power to bring it to pass. Thank You for Your voice and how You speak to us, and for Your passionate heart to see us live an abundant life. Bless our finances and bless our home.

PROPHETIC ACT

Declare this week, "I AM MADE FOR A PURPOSE." (Reference to your Purpose Train).

PURPOSE TRAIN
WORKSHEET

PURPOSE

In the space below, come up with some words and ideas that answer the question, why am I building a Prosperous Home?

Pick one word you wrote that best describes your Purpose and write it here:

____

VISION

In the space below, brainstorm dreams and ideas answering the question, what do I see for my Prosperous Home?

Although you will only have one purpose for your home, you might have multiple visions. For now though, pick one word you wrote that best describes your Vision and write it here: ____________________

STRATEGY

In the space below, list some ways on how you will achieve a Prosperous Home?

Always try to simplify your ideas to one word to help bring clarity and help you remember your answers. Write your Strategies here: ____________________

____________________ ____________________ ____________________

TACTICS

Now that you have brought purpose to your Prosperous Home, which Tactical decisions might you need to add, change, or prioritize?

____________________ (1st priority) ____________________ (4th priority)

____________________ (2nd priority) ____________________ (5th priority)

____________________ (3rd priority) ____________________ (6th priority)

NOTES

CHAPTER 03

BALANCE SHEET **DISCOVERY**

The last chapter created a framework for understanding why you are becoming a Prosperous Home. Clarity of purpose is a like a deep rudder—without it, you won't be able to navigate successfully toward the goal of prosperity. It will be easier to see this more clearly as your family moves beyond mere survival and begins to capture and carry wealth well.

A Prosperous Home is achieved on purpose, not by accident. Success, including financial success, is all about doing purpose well. Biblically, success is measured in terms of wealth (see 1 Timothy 6:17). But what is wealth? For Christians, real wealth is Jesus, and Jesus cares most about people and His relationship to people. Therefore, we must overlay that priority on our value system. If we are wealth creators, then we can safely and biblically measure success best when we use our wealth to the advantage of people.

Wealth can be tangible when it deals with matters like cash and investments, or intangible when it deals with matters like blessing and honor. A Prosperous Home values every level of wealth because this is our calling as supernatural stewards (see 1 Corinthians 4:2). I like to illustrate wealth as layers in the Earth, the core being the most important, the surface being less important (but not worthless). Here is a simple wealth map illustration; you can find the expanded version at page 194:[9]

9 *Chapter 13 continues the discussion of true riches over money. Look for the sequel to this manual called Prosperous Home Investor, due out in 2018.*

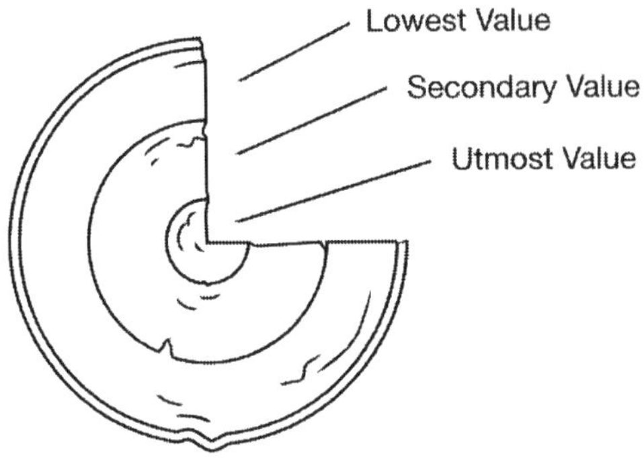

Utmost: True Riches—Peace, Purity, Legacy... (Luke 12:34)
Secondary: Knowledge & Wisdom—Education, Skills, Platform... (Proverbs 16:16)
Lowest: Net Worth—Money, Riches, Possessions... (Proverbs 22:4)

Tangible or measurable wealth is recorded on a balance sheet. The balance sheet is imperfect, but useful as a tool in our service for Christ. As we track our success and progress in terms of assets minus debts, we gain experience with the most important gauge on the control panel of our home. The sum of assets minus debt is called net worth.

+ Assets – Debts = Net Worth

This is the *accounting equation*. Written vertically, you get the same result.

$$\begin{array}{c} + \text{ Assets} \\ - \text{ Debts} \\ \hline = \text{NW} \end{array}$$

This equation lays the foundation for measuring your tangible progress as a steward. Think of your personal finances as an airplane and you are the pilot. Net worth represents altitude, our elevation above ground zero (or literally speaking, zero net worth). If your net worth is zero, you are parked on the runway. If you are extremely busy with your money and your net worth is still zero, you are taxiing around the airport but not actually going anywhere.

Sometimes our net worth falls below zero, into the negative. This is called net deficit. If this is your case, do not despair; Prosperous Home has a solution for you too! For now, take a deep breath and forge ahead. Let's first learn the basics of flying. Then we will tend to your individual circumstances with faith and power. As your net worth gains altitude, you will soon be able to clear the buildings and obstacles around you and fly far as a steward.

Let's begin by constructing your balance sheet to discover where you are regarding your net worth. Remember, net worth is the sum of total assets minus total debts. Let's begin by creating two lists; one for all your assets and one for all your debts.

ASSET LIST

Assets are what you own. Creating your asset list can be daunting, so imagine it from an airplane's 10,000-foot view. From that height, most details are hidden and only the main characteristics are identifiable. This analogy is helpful to keep from bogging down in unnecessary details. You can always refine later. For now, work with your main assets, such as savings, homes, vehicles, and major investments.

Here is a list of assets to stimulate your thinking. If something doesn't look familiar, just overlook it for now and move along without spinning your wheels.

Cash on Hand (available or easily accessible)
Emergency Fund (for unexpected emergencies)
Savings (for planned spending like repairs and replacements)
Retirement (long-term investing for old age)
Vehicles (including cars, trucks, motorcycles, boats, and RVs)
Home (owned, not rented)
Investments (assets held for growth or income)
Land (bare or developed)
Rental Property (second homes or buildings owned by you)
Intellectual Property (created assets like art, books, and music owned by you)

Each of these assets will have a value on the balance sheet. For some, the original price never changes, like cash and savings.[10] But most assets have flexible values over time due to wear, inflation, or value changes. For example, imagine Jim purchases a brand-new vehicle. The price from the manufacturer lists at $45,000, yet the dealership is willing to negotiate down to $40,000. Jim takes the deal, drives it off the lot, and the value immediately falls to $35,000 because it has just become a used car. How does Jim report the car on his balance sheet?

For this course, use today's current value on the balance sheet. Ask yourself, "What is the car worth today?" For Jim, the car is worth $35,000, even though it cost him $40,000 and its manufacturer-suggested retail price (MSRP) was $45,000 only hours before.

Sometimes values go up and not down. For many years, real estate (like land or homes) consistently gained value and certain stocks seemed to defy gravity. Today markets are more volatile, meaning prices continue to rise and fall. Take a moment to create your asset list and include your "best guess" at today's current values. If an asset has a related debt, like a home mortgage or a car loan, list the whole value on the asset list and the debt separately on the debt list. More about debts will follow. For now, add additional lines as needed or disregard any that don't apply. Spend no more than 60 minutes gathering and estimating your assets with values. List your results below.

Your **Assets** Today (at current value):

Cash on Hand	____________	Rental Property	____________
Emergency Fund	____________	Intellectual Property	____________
Savings	____________	Other	____________
Retirement	____________	Other	____________
Vehicles	____________	Land	____________
Home	____________	Investments	____________

SUM the current values and write the total here: ______________

10 *I realize all asset values change over time. But given that this is a basic course, we will accept some generalities to teach principles that can later be refined. Remember, we are soaring at 10,000 feet and not looking at confounding details.*

DEBT LIST

Debts are what you owe. Most families understand they owe money, but they shy away from actually listing them all in one place. This is natural to avoid unhappy news, but ignoring the fact is neither helpful nor wise. A Prosperous Home realizes that God is for you and He already knows your total debt. Gathering it before your eyes takes courage and you have an abundance of that through Christ. Consider it an act of faith, which is pleasing to God.

> *And without faith it is impossible to please Him, for he who comes to God must believe that He is and that He is the rewarder of those who seek Him.*
>
> *Hebrews 11:6 NASB*

As you list every debt, include key information such as the name of the person or entity to which the debt is owed, the balance owed as of today, the interest rate, and estimated minimum payments, if applicable. We will use those later. For now, we will concentrate on the balance owed as of today. List those on the following lines. Remember to include any mortgages or loans secured by assets like homes, cars, and boats. Again, spend no more than 60 minutes gathering and estimating these figures.

Your **Debts** Today (at today's balances)

Credit Card #1	____________	Boats & RV Loans	____________
Credit Card #2	____________	Home Mortgage #1	____________
Credit Card #3	____________	Home Equity Loans	____________
Car Loan #1	____________	Lines of Credit	____________
Car Loan #2	____________	Investment Margin Loans	____________
Other Loans	____________		

SUM the loan balances and write the total here: ____________________

Using the totals above, calculate your **net worth** using the accounting equation

+ Total Assets ____________ - Total Debts ____________ = Net Worth ____________

Congratulations on finding your current net worth. You have just joined the ranks of the educated few! For many, this discovery can be an emotional one. Own the feelings, but limit their influence. If this moment creates feelings of relief and excitement, then press on with your well-earned momentum. If instead you are feeling negative emotions like discouragement, fear, or hopelessness, understand the promise in taking Prosperous Home. This course can be likened to seeing a physician for an injury or disease. You have bravely chosen to end vulnerable cycles and patterns. You have wisely chosen a path forward that gives you power over your circumstances. With the help of your Father in Heaven, you will heal the past and set upon a biblical course for mastering your money and pursuing your purpose.

Place your hand over your heart and draw upon Christ's own prophetic prayer. May it rest upon you like never before to encourage and embolden your Prosperous Home.

> *Our Father who is in heaven, hallowed be Your name. Your kingdom come. Your will be done, on earth as it is in heaven. Give us this day our daily bread. And forgive us our debts, as we also have forgiven our debtors. And do not lead us into temptation, but deliver us from evil. For Yours is the kingdom and the power and the glory forever. Amen.*
>
> *Matthew 6:9-13 NASB*

LESSONS
CHAPTER THREE

HOMEWORK

Copy the numbers you filled out in the chapter on to the Balance Sheet Discovery Exercise found on the next page.

VIDEO

Watch video #3 entitled, "Balance Sheet Discovery," on your DVD or online curriculum.

Watch tutorial video #1 entitled, "Balance Sheet Over Time," on your DVD or online curriculum.

GOING DEEPER

What feelings came up while filling out the balance sheet?

How does the balance sheet help you in understanding your finances?

What methods of home budgeting have you used in the past?

Who do you know who can answer questions about your balance sheet?

How does viewing wealth as more than just money help put in perspective the role or purpose of money?

How would you describe your balance sheet?

How would you like your balance sheet to change?

FURTHER STUDY

Search the Internet and mobile apps for balance sheet examples using the words, "personal Balance Sheet." If you currently use a personal finance software, consider developing its balance sheet data. Listen to Stephen's audio teaching "Financial Keys for Couples."

Read or memorize the following verses: Proverbs 27:23, 1 Corinthians 4:2, 1 Timothy 5:8, 1 Peter 4:10.

PRAYER

Jesus, I trust You with my finances. Thank You for giving me the ability to steward well. Increase my capacity to carry wealth. Show me Your true riches and give me divine wisdom and strategy to increase my net worth in the journey.

PROPHETIC ACT

Pray the Lord's Prayer over your life every day for seven days (See Matthew 6:9-13). Journal any changes you discover.

BALANCE SHEET
DISCOVERY EXERCISE

Your **Assets** Today (at current value):

Cash on Hand	______	Investments	______
Emergency Fund	______	Land	______
Savings	______	Rentals	______
Retirement	______	Intellectual Property	______
Vehicles	______	Other	______
Home	______	Other	______

Total all the assets here: ______________

Your **Debts** Today (at today's balances):

Credit Card #1	______	Home Mortgage	______
Credit Card #2	______	Home Equity Loans	______
Credit Card #3	______	Lines of Credit	______
Car Loan #1	______	Investment Margin Loans	______
Car Loan #2	______	Other Loans	______
Boats & RV Loans	______		

Total all the debts here: ______________

Net Worth: Using the totals above, calculate your net worth using the accounting equation:

+ Total Assets ______________
- Total Debts ______________
=Net Worth ______________

NOTES

CHAPTER 04

THE TARGET BALANCE SHEET

The powerful advantage of understanding a balance sheet is the ability to aim your money the way a pilot navigates toward a destination. Aiming home finances at a purpose is one of the greatest steps toward wealth any family can take. Aim happens when you set an educated and prayerful target for each asset and debt figure on your balance sheet.

Using your figures from last chapter, imagine how the amounts might change given a full year of faithful and successful stewarding. For example, if today's cash is zero, you could target a future cash balance of $5,000. If a credit card balance today totals $5,000, you could target a future balance of zero. Line by line, intentionally work through your balance sheet and set a new target for each figure one year from now.

The two examples I just gave require a change of $10,000, which will come directly out of your Living category (more on this in Chapter 6). Realize that many balances won't change. Small changes are just as important as large ones, so take care not to exaggerate your capacity for this target exercise. Each change should be realistic, based on your best knowledge of what you can achieve. If you are married, set these targets as a couple in full agreement. If you have children, consider ways to involve them so they can participate and learn about setting targets.

It is fun to dream and imagine what God can do, but for this exercise, only plan what you can reasonably expect considering current circumstances. This is not a dream exercise, but it is a stewardship exercise. Exercise your faithfulness as a steward and build good targets. Of course we ask for God's supernatural increase, but once we've asked, what remains for us is to steward between the miracles. For this exercise, only estimate balance sheet targets that you can manage, given your best guess and faithfulness of incomes now. This is what Jesus means by being "faithful in a very little thing":

> *"And he said to him, 'Well done, good slave, because you have been faithful in a very little thing, you are to be in authority over ten cities.'"*
>
> *Luke 19:17 NASB*

On the next page is a sample balance sheet. Column 1 shows this person's assets and debts as of today. Column 2 shows the line-by-line, best-guess targets for every asset and debt. Notice that not every line changes. This shows which assets and debts the person has chosen to focus on improving.

Also, notice that the home mortgage and auto loans improve only by small amounts; this is happening through the regular monthly schedule of payments. For many loans, a portion of each payment is split between a balance reduction (called the principal) and the cost of borrowing (called the interest expense). This family has shown the effect of scheduled principal payments without making it a target. Instead, their efforts will be focused on building savings and reducing the credit card balances. Column 3 shows the change in each line. The totals for each column indicate assets minus debts, or net worth. Column 3 shows the changes between each balance and totals to the overall change in net worth. This person's target will require a change of approximately $7,825 to support their one-year plan.

	TODAY'S BALANCE SHEET	TARGET AFTER 1 YEAR	CHANGES BY LINE
Cash on Hand	$400	$400	$0
Emergency Cash	$0	$1,000	$1,000
Savings for a New Car	$200	$1,200	$1,000
Toyota Car	$4,000	$4,000	$0
Chevy Pickup	$8,500	$8,500	$0
Jewelry	$1,000	$1,000	$0
Furniture & Antiques	$2,500	$2,500	$0
Home	$200,000	$201,000	$1,000
IRA Retirement Savings	$2,000	$2,000	$0
401k Retirement Savings	$900	$1,900	$1,000
TOTAL ASSETS	**$219,500**	**$223,500**	**$4,000**
Chase Credit Card	$1,900	$0	-$1,900
VISA Credit Card	$3,900	$3,800	-$100
MasterCard	$425	$0	-$425
Toyota Car Loan	$4,500	$4,300	-$200
Chevy Pickup Loan	$8,100	$7,900	-$200
Home Mortgage	$149,000	$148,000	-$1,000
TOTAL DEBTS	**$167,825**	**$164,000**	**-$3,825**
NET WORTH	**$51,675**	**$59,500**	**$7,825**

A PERSONAL EXAMPLE

When I began creating my own Column 2 targets, cash was very tight and debt was growing. I had zero room for emergencies and I hated owing so much on my credit cards and mortgages. As a result, my first few year's Column 3 changes were very small. I had to resist feeling discouraged, and so might you. We can fight discouragement because we understand these steps are the path to a Prosperous Home. Taking small steps now can lead to great leaps ahead as God adds His strength to your plan faithfully lived out.

As a starting point, I chose to create a small emergency fund. An emergency fund works like a bumper to protect you from unknown but common surprises that steal money from your life. The emergency fund grew to $500 over several months. While I targeted the savings, I gave myself temporary permission to make only the minimum debt payments required on my credit cards. It was slow, I admit, but every time extra money came into my hands I knew right where to put it—my emergency fund. Having a focus on savings resolved the anxiety I felt over carrying debt. I knew that once I had my $500 savings in place, I would be better protected against unknown emergencies.

But what comes after you reach your desired cash level? For me, cash grew in stages because I alternated back and forth between building emergency funds and paying off debts. I worked at a simple swing between increasing cash and paying down debt, and each of these swings drove net worth higher. Though conventional wisdom says to pay debt off "at all costs," in the beginning I found that was not sound advice. Without an adequate emergency fund, I was vulnerable to perpetuating my debt no matter how hard I tried to escape. In an emergency, my debt reductions made little advantage, because I was caught in a debt cycle that relied upon credit in an emergency. (While I teach the idea of growing cash or paying down debt as alternatives, please understand that you can adapt the idea however you need.)

Every car has a bumper. There is a common-sense reason for that. The same logic applies with an emergency fund. Build your savings little by little, and begin with a conservative emergency fund target. This Target Balance Sheet is a powerful way to escape a debt cycle. This is the same tool you will use to gain altitude with your home, and create net worth that can overcome those unknown but foreseeable emergencies that threaten us all. This is faithful stewardship, and it is pleasing to God.

Moreover it is required in stewards, that a man be found faithful.

1 Corinthians 4:2 CWS

The next chapter will introduce the economic funnel, the cash flow equation, and the three types of income that support net worth. In the chapter following that, we see how spending can be strategically aimed at assets or debt relief.

LESSONS

CHAPTER FOUR

HOMEWORK

Fill out the Target Balance Sheet found on the next page.

VIDEO

Watch video #4 entitled, "The Target Balance Sheet," on your DVD or online curriculum.

Watch tutorial video #2 entitled, "Change in Net Worth," on your DVD or online curriculum.

Watch tutorial video #3 entitled, "Financial Story Slideshow," on your DVD or online curriculum.

GOING DEEPER

How does your Purpose Train help you create goals for your Target Balance Sheet?

What are some ways you have included your children in your financial decisions?

How can you train your children to be successful in handling money?

How have you navigated disappointment and setbacks in the past?

How does creating goals help you aim at something and have purpose in your day-to-day decisions?

What ways have you seen God come through for you in your finances?

FURTHER STUDY

Read or memorize these verses: Deuteronomy 15:6, Proverbs 22:7, Luke 12:43, Luke 22:36.

Listen to Stephen's message entitled "Wealth Factor."

Search the Internet for these subjects: sudden wealth syndrome, war on poverty, wealth by nations, debt by nation, and global wealth.

PRAYER

Father God, I am excited for this journey to gain power over my finances. Bless me in this process and help me as I bring purpose to my finances. Give me wisdom and direction for my finances and favor to accomplish my goals.

PROPHETIC ACT

Create a list of 100 dreams you hope to achieve in your lifetime. These need not be financial in nature.

TARGET

BALANCE SHEET

	TODAY'S BALANCE SHEET	TARGET AFTER 1 YEAR	CHANGES BY LINE
Cash on Hand			
Emergency Cash			
Savings for a New Car			
Car #1			
Car #2			
Jewelry			
Furniture & Antiques			
Home			
IRA Retirement Savings			
401k Retirement Savings			
TOTAL ASSETS			
Credit Card #1			
Credit Card #2			
Credit Card #3			
Car Loan #1			
Car Loan #2			
Home Mortgage			
TOTAL DEBTS			
NET WORTH			

NOTES

CHAPTER

05

THE HOME ECONOMY

Every home has a system of inflows and outflows. The Prosperous Home's economy can be written as a cash flow equation where inflows of all sources equal outflows for all reasons. Simply stated, inflows equal outflows.

Inflows = Outflows

Notice how this equation balances 100% of all the money. This is different than other financial courses which follow traditional accounting principles using the equation: Income – Expense = Profit. That is a residual model that adapts very well for business, but not so well for homes.[11]

Let's begin with the inflow side of the equation. The term inflow is broader than income. For example, all incomes are inflows, but not all inflows are income. This means some inflows are not income.

11 *For my accounting-savvy students, Prosperous Home lessons align closer to the statement of cash flows than the income statement. I chose this approach to better teach a basic grasp of net worth. This course is designed to bring complex ideas into focus for non-accountants. I believe its wisdom will become self-evident as it bears fruit for my students. See Matthew 11:19b.*

In the U.S., we are only taxed when inflows come from income. That is why it's called an "income tax." This seemingly small distinction is very important to understand because some inflows are not taxable; only income is taxed. Borrowed money is one example of an inflow that is not income. This is the reason we are not taxed when we borrow money or use our credit cards.

One of the great threats to a Prosperous Home occurs when a family borrows to make ends meet. They mix income with borrowing to balance their cash flow equation. If inflows = outflows but you are borrowing to balance your equation, you will find yourself on a precarious path, one that should not continue. We will discuss borrowing in a later chapter, but for now, I want to lay the foundation that some inflows are not sound when building a Prosperous Home.

Another example of an inflow that is not income is money raised from selling an asset. These dollars are not an increase, but simply a return of your original investment. It is not income, therefore is it not taxable.[12] Of course, we hope our investments grow. If and investment does grow in value and you get more back than you originally invested, the increase is called a "gain" and is taxed as income. But only the increase (or decrease) is a tax item, not the recovery of original investment.

INCREASE IMPLIES INCOME

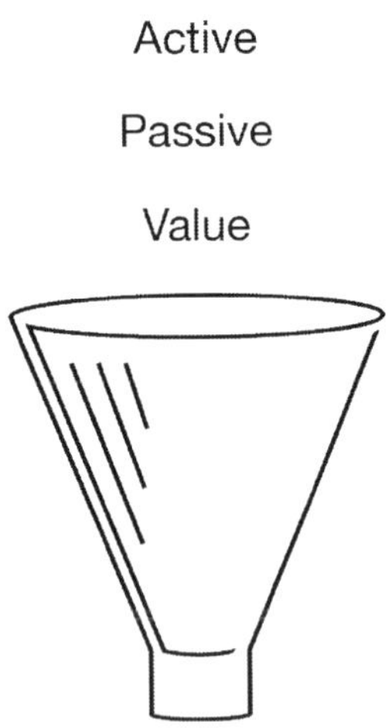

Increase implies income because increase has the potential to add new money onto a home balance sheet. The idea of increase is found both biblically and in American tax law. Wages and salaries are common examples of increase; they are also the most common way for homes to grow.

Actually, there are three types of increase. They are called active, passive, and value income.

12 *This is known as "Basis" in tax and accounting theory.*

ACTIVE INCOME

Active income is money earned in exchange for your time, knowledge, and skill. This includes wages, salaries, and self-employment earnings.

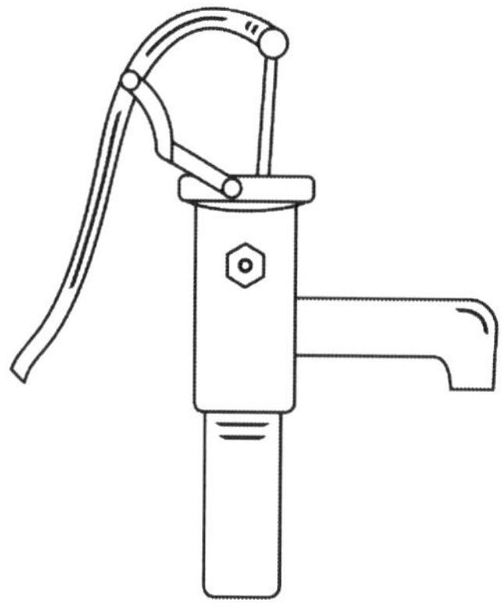

The nature of active income is like a water pump; as long as the person pumps the handle, money continues to flow. For example, consider the employee. She has some skill or knowledge that an employer wants. The employee sells her time in exchange for a paycheck. There is a sense of stability for the hourly worker, provided the employment is acceptable and the employer is satisfied. The employee is effectively working for money.

Most American homes are supported in this way. Here are some familiar examples of active income[13] streams you may recognize:

Jobs and better jobs
Raises and bonuses
Benefits
Sales and Commissions
Self-employment businesses (manufacturing, sales, and services)
Multi-level marketing (MLM) businesses
Preaching, missionary, and itinerant ministries
Gambling, sports, and non-traditional models, i.e. trading and antiquing

Each of these streams of are viewed by our federal (and some state and local government) agencies as earned income. Earned income is the most heavily-taxed type of increase a person can have to support a home. As a person grows in their sophistication with money, they tend to replace earned income with lesser-taxed inflows. That discussion falls beyond the scope of Prosperous Home, but I look forward to sharing more in my sequel, Prosperous Home Investor.

---

13 *Some phrases are borrowed from Bethel Church original offering readings to show how much we say is rooted almost subconsciously in a working class ideology. See www.bethelredding.org/offering-readings for more examples of offering declarations.*

Most Americans rely on employment for their primary streams of income. Part-time workers might juggle two or three jobs to manage their family's spending. When those jobs or small business incomes are interrupted, serious conditions arise. Under-employment is a serious threat to a home and a perennial problem around the world. Life is sometimes unpredictable and incomes rise and fall. A Prosperous Home understands this reality and plans accordingly. A powerful way to posture for the unexpected is by adding more streams of income flowing into the home. This is easier than it may appear, as we understand there are other types of income.

PASSIVE INCOME

Previously, I used a water pump to illustrate how active income continues as long as we are actively pumping. If I work the handle by showing up every day, the income continues to flow. Passive income works differently, like an artesian well that bubbles freely from the earth. Because the income flows without my continual pumping, my bucket fills even when I'm resting.

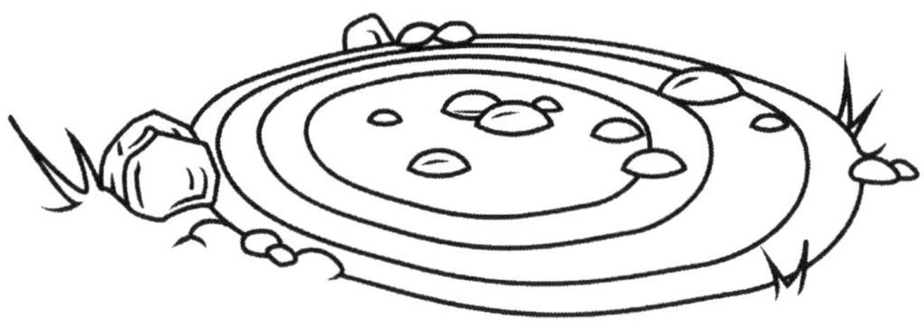

Going further, passive income stacks better than active income. This means two or three active incomes are likely all a home can manage because of the time and energy required. But families can stack as many passive income streams as they can find without toiling; passive incomes demand little effort once they begin to flow. This frees you to build another, and then another passive stream. What a powerful model to consider as you advance through life and attempt to multiply your income streams. Finally, passive income is taxed at a lower rate than earned (active) income.

This means more of every dollar comes into your hand instead of leaking away as taxes. Here are some examples of passive income streams:

Royalties and advances (authored works like music, art, and books)
Mineral royalties (crude oil, natural gas, and mining)
Commodity royalties (wheat, water, and harvests)
Interest income
Dividend income
Rental income

VALUE STREAMS

Earlier I mentioned something about old investment money. While that money is working, the value of your investment may grow. This is the third type of income stream, flowing from the changes in values. Just as a river changes and grows, the value of your investments and assets will change and grow. Some assets are purchased and held over time because they are expected to gain in value or pay passive income. The money used to make longer and larger investments is referred to as capital and forms the basis for the idea of capitalism—the use of assets as capital to make more capital.

Capital is an accumulation of money that is pooled and invested beyond your daily living need. Capital is where businesses, infrastructure, and long-term wealth come from. Capitalism implies calculated risks over many years. Capital is the very thing that transforms income into inheritances and impoverished villages into wealthy nations.

From Genesis to Revelation, the Bible is filled with language and principles supporting God's esteem for capital. Capital tends to imply large values, but for Prosperous Home students, your long-term savings, real estate holdings, personal residence, and retirement savings can all be viewed as capital. Because capital spans time, capital values will move up and down. These changes measure the third and final type of income we call value streams. When capital investments are sold, the gains in value create income, while the losses of value consume it.

Capital in the form of stocks, bonds, and mutual funds trades continuously on exchanges like NYSE and NASDAQ. These massive financial systems measure value changes in microseconds and fractional cents. Other capital values change more slowly and bluntly, like collectables and antiques. How a person refines their investments is a subject beyond the scope of Prosperous Home. Look for those discussions in my sequel, Prosperous Home Investor. For now, understand that how you invest over time may increase or deplete capital, and selling those investments can cause those changes to be realized in what I am calling value streams.

Here are some examples of value income streams:

Gains (minus losses) on stocks, bonds, and mutual fund investments
Gains (minus losses) on vehicles, boats, and recreational vehicles (RVs)
Gains (minus losses) on real estate like homes, land, and rental properties
Gains (minus losses) on the composite values of businesses and partnerships
Gains (minus losses) on appraised values for creative works and future income streams
Gains (minus losses) on sales of art, collectibles, and antiques
Gains (minus losses) on sales of gold, metal, and commodity holdings
Gains (minus losses) on sales of tangible or intangible assets that are marketable

TOTALING ALL YOUR INCOME STREAMS

The totals of these income streams represents a reasonable approximation of monthly income that you are using to support your lifestyle. As I explained at the beginning of this chapter, the total omits other inflows like borrowing because we are measuring the income's ability to support outflows. Now, you will fill out your own worksheet at the end of this chapter evaluating your income streams. After that, we will shift to the spending side of the cash flow equation and compare the inflows and outflows. From there we create a plan to support your Target Balance Sheet.

LESSONS
CHAPTER FIVE

HOMEWORK

Fill out the Active, Passive, & Value Income Worksheet found on the next page.

VIDEO

Watch video #5 entitled, "The Home Economy," on your DVD or online curriculum.

Watch tutorial video #4, "Inflows Equal Outflows," on your DVD or online curriculum.

Watch tutorial video #5, "Three Types of Income," on your DVD or online curriculum.

GOING DEEPER

What feelings came up while filling out your Basic Income Sheet?

How does balancing the equation, inflow = outflow, change your view of your finances?

How does viewing income as active, passive, and value raise your ideas of increasing your net worth?

What are some ways you can increase your income stream?

What is a dream job and a dream income for you and your family?

Create a list of 100 items for which you are thankful.

FURTHER STUDY

Read or memorize these verses: Luke 10:7, Proverbs 31:16.
Listen to Stephen's message entitled "Financial Keys for New Couples."

Search the Internet for these subjects: active income, passive income, and types of intellectual property.

Find other examples of church offering readings and create your own based on scripture and faith.

PRAYER

Jesus, thank You for the ability to create wealth. Thank You for the income streams You have given me. I ask You for wisdom and strategy for multiplying and increasing streams of income in my life.

PROPHETIC ACT

Choose a scripture to declare over your finances every day this week. Journal any noticeable changes you or others experience.

ACTIVE, PASSIVE, & VALUE
INCOME WORKSHEET

Active Income Streams:

Job #1 Gross Wages (before taxes) ____________________
Job #2 Gross Wages (before taxes) ____________________
Job #3 Gross Wages (before taxes) ____________________
Small Business #1 (net after expenses) ____________________
Small Business #2 (net after expenses) ____________________
Small Business #3 (net after expenses) ____________________
Winning and Prizes ____________________

Passive Income Streams:

Interest Income #1 ____________________
Interest Income #2 ____________________
Dividend Income #1 ____________________
Dividend Income #2 ____________________
Rental Income #1 ____________________
Rental Income #2 ____________________
Royalty Income #1 ____________________
Royalty Income #2 ____________________

Net Value Changes: ____________________

TOTAL INCOME ____________________

NOTES

CHAPTER 06

THE SPENDING **SIDE OF LGS**

In the last chapter I introduced the inflows = outflows equation and introduced the types of income streams available for cash flow. Making the claim that inflows equal outflows can fuel anxiety for those struggling through tight economic seasons. If that's you, here is some encouragement.

First, remember that seasons always "come to pass." Admittedly, some seasons stay longer than others, but life has a way of cycling, and yours will soon bring you through. Your current circumstances offer a great advantage for learning how to steward even small amounts. This is a biblical principle working on your behalf that leads to reward. Building sound spending habits in the down times will leverage in multiples when breakthrough comes. Watch our Father in heaven bless and promote you to His delight as you steward your financial times now in faith.

> *"'Well done, my good servant!' his master replied. 'Because you have been trustworthy in a very small matter, take charge of ten cities.'"*
>
> *Luke 19:17 NIV*

Think back to good times past. It might not have been too many months ago when you had the money needed. You bought the car or rented the home. You had enough to get new clothes for school or even give generously to some important need. Most of us have experienced good times and there are lessons hidden in that fact. First, don't let the bad times steal hope and gratitude for those good times. Allow this course to forge new thinking, so that when the next wave of breakthrough comes, you can build better. Soon you will fly above your financial trials like an airplane above a storm; you will soar because God wants you to prosper. Remember your Purpose Train exercise? Review those pages now and allow this prayer to lift your gaze.

Father in heaven, I pray for Your help to interrupt and improve my circumstances. I press hard into Your good hope and order the silence of worries that cloud my thinking. Break through to me, Father. I await Your rescue. I ask all this by faith in Jesus Christ. Amen.

SPENDING

All spending should compliment your Purpose Train. In fact, every dollar you spend needs to advance the Purpose, Vision, and Strategy of your life. Eliminating any spending that does not contribute to your momentum can solve what has become, for many, the greatest puzzle in the home.

Spending can be either proactive or reactive. Proactive means intentional spending in alignment with your Purpose Train; reactive means accidental, incidental, or disengaged spending that continues until something bad happens to make you feel victimized.

Proactive = Spending on purpose
Reactive = Spending on accident

Many Americans are reactive in their spending. They disengage from financial diligence and spend as urgencies and opportunities present themselves. They avoid financial matters to the point of harm. Harm can be minor, like the gnawing fear of making ends meet, or major, such as repossessions, foreclosures, and bankruptcies. Sometimes harm is unavoidable—as I've said, life is unpredictable. But even with life's volatility, I observe that most financial harms are self-inflicted and preventable with proactive spending.

Proactive spending begins with the simple tool called LGS. LGS stands for Living, Giving, and Saving—meaning every outflow can be placed into one of these three broad categories. I'll write the cash flow equation again using the LGS spending categories.

Inflows = Living + Giving + Saving

In Chapter 5, I illustrated income as arrows flowing into an income pool (Illustration Y). Now imagine that pool as the top of a funnel. Every income stream of the household —grouped as either active, passive, or value income—flows into the top. The streams first move through the widest part of the funnel, which represents the widest part of our spending: Living. The narrow part of the funnel represents our Giving, and the drip from the bottom represents our Saving, which methodically and mechanically fills the bucket known as net worth.

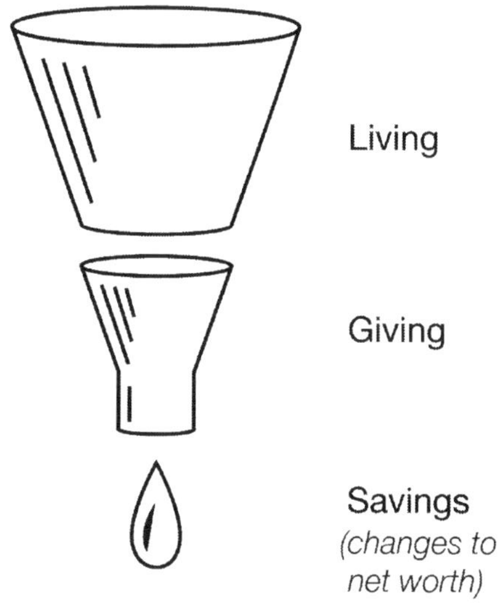

Every dollar that enters the funnel (inflows) must go to one of these three categories:

> Living is the category for all spending related to housing, personal, auto, health, education, taxes, and entertainment;
> Giving is the category for all spending related to church tithes, pledges paid, offerings, and other gifts;
> Saving is the category for growing net worth by increasing assets or reducing debts.

The Living category is the widest, carrying most of the costs associated with your lifestyle. Choices to change spending in the Living category can contribute greatly toward balancing a home's cash flow equation. Because the Living category is the largest category, it often yields many small reductions that combine to a big relief each month.

Without the help of your Purpose Train, cuts to the Living category can trigger feelings of defeat and discouragement. Help yourself by viewing potential cuts through the Purpose Train like a lens. Cut or reduce any spending that does not contribute to why you are alive.

Be quick to manage any sense of loss or discouragement you might feel when ending certain spending patterns. You are developing a proactive approach to spending, and this new skill exercises clarity of purpose. Those old feelings are what led you into reactive spending in the first place. They are like painted lines on a road, guiding your spending using comfort and convenience rather than identity and purpose. Looking down, you follow lines that go nowhere; looking up, you engage vision and make progress. This is true in the natural and it is true for money.

All spending that remains find its source in who you are. It is refreshing to discover that using money on things that really matter is a powerful part of engineering a life "in Christ." Lifestyle is the product of our own creative power. This is one small way we demonstrate what it means to be made in our Creator's image. Like Him, we shape much of the world around us[14]. Often our world is a demonstration of what lies within us. Order manifests order, but chaos manifests chaos. Our responsibility for both internal and external worlds may be challenging for some people to accept, especially when life seems out of control. But we are empowered to do good, and God will help us in that endeavor.

A sage friend once explained that there are only three characters in every great piece of literature, and these same exist within us: the victim, the villain, and the hero. The victim is the one who is powerless and to whom life happens. The villain has power, but uses it wrongly to bully others. The hero is the one who, through courage and hope, changes the world around him or herself for good. Heroes are agents of righteousness and catalysts for change without excuse or manipulation. You are that hero for your Prosperous Home.

---

14 *In this thinking, I stop short of the fallacy that we can "think and grow rich." We are not gods, though some have wrongly taught us otherwise. More on this doctrinal misstep is available in my Prosperous Soul Foundations Manual.*

LIVING WITHIN YOUR MEANS

Many financial educators talk about living within your means. For many Americans, that means living at the limits of your income. However, this idea is incomplete. If we consider this "living within your means" idea through the lens of Living, Giving, Saving (LGS), it would mean spending 100% in the following way:

L	100%
G	0%
S	0%
	100%

Recalling the funnel illustration, this means 100% of income flowing into the family is all spent in the Living category. This treats all income like bread that should be consumed by the family in the short term. In contrast, a Prosperous Home perceives LGS spending like bread and seed. Living is the bread, and Giving and Saving are the seed. Bread is the part we eat, and seed is the part we plant. Bread makes us stronger, healthier, and more stable; seed makes the way for a better tomorrow.

The idea of bread and seed deepens the argument of living within your means. Everyone understands you must plant seed in order to get bread. Likewise, the LGS model envisions spending for both bread and seed. It is not enough to spend 100% on Living; rather, we need spending to span both bread and seed to truly live within our means. For a Prosperous Home, living within your means might begin like this:

L	80%
G	10%
S	10%
	100%

Notice that Living costs are set at 80%, and both Giving and Saving are matched at 10% each. This LGS of 80/10/10 is a great start at dividing your spending between bread and seed. Spending into your seed first (Giving/Saving) and living on what remains is a biblical application of the idea "pay yourself first."

As Christians, we are called to live for God. That sounds so grand and spiritual, but really it is very plain and common for a believer. Godly living is hidden in the day-to-day rhythm of work and play. The way we care for ourselves and others matters to God. The opportunities for kindness and bravery are constant. Forgiveness, humility, perseverance, creativity—these and myriad other virtues are the brick and mortar that build a pleasing life for Christ. And strangely, our Father in heaven watches to reward us. He lets us enjoy the fruits of our labor. These fruit are what I call bread. It is how we make a stable life and position ourselves as towers of strength. Here are some verses on the idea of bread:

> *And without faith it is impossible to please Him, for he who comes to God must believe that He is and that He is a rewarder of those who seek Him.*
>
> *Hebrews 11:6 NASB*

> *For the Scripture says, "You shall not muzzle the on while he is threshing," and "The laborer is worthy of his wages."*
>
> *1 Timothy 5:18 NASB*

GIVING OF TITHE AND OFFERING

Giving includes all your generosity spending, from international donations to the hungry man asking for a sandwich. The subject of giving is complicated and emotional so here we will view it from the 10,000-foot view. All giving can be divided into two categories called tithe and offering.

Tithes are given to support your local church.
Offerings are given to support everything else.

The modern idea of tithing is rooted in the Jewish rabbinical laws called maaser. Maaser is a law that requires Jews to give the first ten percent of their income to support the priests and teachers of the Torah. These traditional targets of priests, synagogues, and religious schools have been compared in our culture to the home church and pastoral staff. This comparison makes sense because most of our spiritual growth comes at the hand of faithful pastors and teachers.

The word tithe means tenth, so if someone is giving 10% or less, their giving belongs to the tithe. If someone gives more than 10%, then the amount above ten represents something else. Above ten percent is where offerings begin.

Offerings are optional and self-directed in our Western culture. Offering dollars should be given to support missions, missionaries, or any other qualified charitable spending where you feel God's pleasure. Consider in advance where to put your offerings. Remember, all giving is seed, and you should know what you're planting. Learn how to say yes and no, especially in the areas of giving. Never sow carelessly; needs are real and serious, so place your money well as a Prosperous Home.

I have much more to say about giving, but will defer to my forthcoming book about the tithe. For now, I offer the following two thoughts. First, the Bible is clear in both Old and New Testaments that tithing is a source of blessing. In Malachi, God says to test Him and see the truth of this. And in the New Testament Jesus scolds the Pharisees for performing the law of tithing but neglecting the more important issues of justice, mercy, and faithfulness. In the end, Jesus Himself affirms both the important issues as well as the tithe:

> *"Bring the whole tithe into the storehouse, so that there may be food in My house, and test Me now in this," says the LORD of hosts, "if I will not open for you the windows of heaven and pour out for you a blessing until it overflows."*
>
> *Malachi 3:10 NASB*

> *"Woe to you, scribes and Pharisees, hypocrites! For you tithe mint and dill and cumin, and have neglected the weightier provisions of the law: justice and mercy and faithfulness; but these are the things you should have done without neglecting the others."*
>
> *Matthew 23:23 NASB*

Second, our earliest recorded tithe comes from the ancient tradition established by Abram and confirmed later by his descendants Isaac and Jacob. Historically, tithing predates even Abram. It was common in those days for Bedouin tribes to pay a tribute before crossing into another tribal territory. The tribute represented an honorarium, a tax, and a pledge of peace all wrapped together when a tribe was passing through. If the tribute was not paid at the time of crossing, the tribe effectively declared war against the residents of the territory.

This is exactly the significance of Abram's first tithe. If you read the passage in context, he and his cadre of 318 men are returning home after successfully rescuing Abram's nephew, Lot, from the armies of four kings, who had themselves defeated and plundered five other kings. Abram and his fighters had pursued these armies into faraway lands, and on the journey home, the road brought them upon the boundary of a certain great king named Melchizedek. This king was very different from others because he was both king and priest. His kingdom was called Salem (which means peace), and he served a single God known as "Most High" in a time of polytheism. Oh, and one more thing: Melchizedek had no beginning or end of life, no parents, and no genealogy. He was a foreshadowing or type of Jesus Christ:

> *Without father, without mother, without genealogy, having neither beginning of days nor end of life but made like the Son of God, he remains a priest perpetually.*
>
> *Hebrews 7:3 NASB*

I imagine Abram paused at the boundary of this unexplored land. Before him stood the King of Peace, while behind him were 318 weary fighters and all the bounty won back from nine kings (the four he pursued plus the five that were pillaged). He made a choice to honor the God who caused this miracle to happen. Abram paid a tribute, one tenth of all the increase. But what is new is Abram's worship to this God Most High. Abram became the world's first monotheist, and the Hebrew nation was born in the act—a simple tribute paid to avoid war with an eternal Priest, and to acknowledge his singular worship of the Almighty God.

> *And Melchizedek king of Salem brought out bread and wine; now he was a priest of God Most High. He blessed him and said, "Blessed be Abram of God Most High, Possessor of heaven and earth; And blessed be God Most High, Who has delivered your enemies into your hand." He gave him a tenth of all.*
>
> *Genesis 14:18-20*

For this Melchizedek, king of Salem, priest of the Most High God, who met Abraham as he was returning from the slaughter of the kings and blessed him, to whom also Abraham apportioned a tenth part of all the spoils, was first of all, by the translation of his name, king of righteousness, and then also king of Salem, which is king of peace.

Hebrews 7:1-2

I believe giving is a marvelous act of worship and acknowledgement for the Prosperous Home. How you give and whom you support is between you and God. I encourage you to give something and never withhold the important aspect of planting seed, especially at the boundary of your spiritual journey across the unexplored lands of life. We stand before our King and Priest, Jesus. Offer something.

LESSONS
CHAPTER SIX

HOMEWORK

Using the numbers you wrote in the chapter, fill out the Living, Giving, Saving (LGS) Worksheet on the next page.

VIDEO

Watch video #6 entitled, "The Spending Side of LGS," on your DVD or online curriculum.

Watch tutorial video #6 entitled, "Calculating an LGS Percentage," on your DVD or online curriculum.

Watch tutorial video #7 entitled, "LGS and the Black Swan," on your DVD or online curriculum.

GOING DEEPER

What surprises or realizations came up as you filled out your current LGS?

How would funneling every dollar spent through your Purpose Train help you?

What have been your spending habits in the past?

Why can there be no residual money and every dollar must go into Living, Giving, or Saving?

How do savings change the balance sheet?

How have you seen the idea that what is inside you manifests outside you play out in your life, or in others' lives?

Do you identify more with the victim, villain, or hero? How so?

FURTHER STUDY

Read or memorize these verses: Malachi 3:10-12, Luke 19:17, Hebrews 11:6, 1 Timothy 5:18.

If you don't tithe, pray about testing God for 90 days. Faithfully sow and watch to see what God may do to "rebuke the devourer" and "open the windows of heaven" in your life.

PRAYER

Father God, You are the giver of good gifts. Thank You for all that You have given me. Thank You for using different financial seasons in my life to bring me closer to You. Help me as I bring purpose and intentionality to my finances. Thank You for the courage to be honest and to see clearly where my money is spent.

PROPHETIC ACT

Spend 30 minutes recalling and being thankful for prosperous seasons from the past. Journal the result of that time.

LIVING, GIVING, SAVINGS

(LGS) WORKSHEET

	CURRENT ($)	CURRENT (%)
LIVING		
GIVING		
SAVING		
TOTAL		

	YEAR 1 TARGET ($)	YEAR 1 TARGET (%)
LIVING		
GIVING		
SAVING		
TOTAL		

	DREAM ($)	DREAM (%)
LIVING		
GIVING		
SAVING		
TOTAL		

NOTES

CHAPTER 07

SAVING CHANGES THE BALANCE SHEET

The final category is Saving, which is broader than simply depositing money in a bank. For the LGS, saving consists of any money dripping from the funnel that increases your net worth. Remember the balance sheet equation?

+ Assets
- Debts
= NW

Imagine the balance sheet like a kitchen sink and the funnel like a faucet. Net worth will increase when money flows into the sink (balance sheet) and this flow is what I am loosely calling Saving. We can use that flow either to add assets or to reduce debt; both ways, net worth gets higher. Even if your lifestyle could only dribble 1¢ through the funnel, it would fall into the sink and net worth would grow higher by 1¢. This 1¢ idea will give every family hope that they can improve their balance sheet even in difficult circumstances. If your home has experienced an empty sink, it takes as little as 1¢ to improve your net worth. You can do this. Anyone can improve their balance sheet by simply allowing something to flow through their funnel and onto their balance sheet. Creating a plan that consistently grows net worth is not beyond your reach—it simply requires a plan.

Most kitchen sinks have two sides and the same goes for the balance sheet—the left side is for assets, and the right side is for debts. Now imagine the funnel like the faucet running water into the sink. The size of the stream reflects the size of your saving percentage. I can aim the faucet on either side of the sink. I swing it left so it pours into assets such as emergency funds and other investments, or I can swing it right and make extra payments until I am debt-free. Both methods drive net worth higher. The approach you choose is a mixture of science and personal preference.

In my own home, I first swung the faucet left to create a small emergency fund of $100. When we achieved that goal, I asked God where to aim the faucet next. Debt was my next target so I swung my Saving stream to the right in the form of extra payments on credit card balances. Within a few months, these extra payments were enough to pay off one small credit card balance.

As time passed I swung my Saving stream back and forth between assets and debt, incrementally increasing my emergency fund and eliminating credit card balances. Over time, this approach was vindicated because it leveraged a tiny savings flow into a strong emergency fund equal to the unexpected emergencies that arose. At the same time, small credit card balances were peeling away, creating a snowball effect that fed the Saving stream. We will talk more about debt reduction in Chapter 14. For now, I just share my beginning steps toward building net worth so you can get a picture of how the balance sheet captures your aving stream at the bottom of the cash flow funnel.

SUGGESTIONS FOR CALCULATING YOUR CURRENT LGS

Calculating your current LGS is simple. Work backwards if you need, using the equation: inflows = Living + Giving + Saving. For example, if you know your total income and you have just enough to live, it is likely your Living equals your income. For example, this LGS might look as follows (for simplicity I'll presume a cash flow equation of $1,000 inflows = $1,000 outflows):

L	$1,000	100%
G	$0	0%
S	$0	0%
Total	$1,000	100%

If you borrowed to get through the month and didn't pay it off, then your equation will look like this (Note: borrowing is negative savings because money flows backwards from the balance sheet to support the Living category):

L	$1,100	110%
G	$0	0%
S	<$100>	<10%>
Total	$1,000	100%

If you are a tither, giving 10% of income, then your equation will look like this:

L	$900	90%
G	$100	10%
S	$0	0%
Total	$1,000	100%

If you borrowed to pay the tithe, then your equation will look like this (Note: borrowing to pay tithe is like sowing seed in another's field):

L	$1,000	100%
G	$100	10%
S	<$100>	<10%>
Total	$1,000	100%

Notice that every total matches the inflows ($1,000 in this case) and the percentages equal 100%. This will always be the case, so use your total income to discover your actual LGS. Take figures from last month, or choose a different month if needed, to get a realistic picture of your norm. Estimate where needed; the goal here is not precision but illustration. Illustrate each line below using your best view at 10,000 feet.

L	$________
G	$________
S	$________
Total	$________

MORE SUGGESTIONS ON CALCULATING YOUR CURRENT LGS

If your credit card balances increase in the month, it is likely your spending is greater than your income by the amount of debt you added. Giving is usually an easy amount to estimate because we tend to donate one or two times a month.

Remember to estimate actual figures from 10,000 feet and don't get bogged down with details. We will work with exact numbers later.

Prove your figures by totaling amounts for Living, Giving, and Saving. This total should equal all income for the month. If it does not, climb back to 10,000 feet and study your numbers. If something is out of whack, borrowing more than you realized is the most likely cause.

Remember, borrowing acts like an inflow, but it is really negative savings.

Income = Living + Giving + Saving

When your figures make sense, convert the LGS into percentages. Doing this is simple with the help of a calculator. Divide the Living amount by the total spending, and you get the Living percentage. Write that percentage to the right of Living amount above.

Next, divide the Giving amount by the total spending, and write that percentage to the right of the Giving amount above.

Next, divide the Saving amount by the total spending, and write that percentage to the right of the Saving amount above.

Finally, add up the three percentages to verify the sum of 100%. If they do not equal 100%, recalculate the amounts and round to ignore decimals.

Here are sample calculations, presuming monthly LGS amounts with a total of $3,000.

L	$2,700	90%
G	$240	8%
S	$60	2%
Total	$3,000	100%

The Living percentage is 90% ($2,700/$3,000=.90 or 90%);
The Giving percentage is 8% ($240/$3,000=.08 or 8%);
The Saving percentage is 2% ($60/$3,000=.02 or 2%);
The Total percentage is 100% (90%+8%+2%=100%).

MORE ON GIVING AND SAVING

Giving is of vital importance to a Prosperous Home because it recognizes our place as strength-givers in a world of needs. The virtue of giving is clear, whether or not you live as a follower of Jesus. Even unbelieving authors and worldly wealth coaches recognize the importance of generosity. Giving is considered one of the fundamental switches for turning on wealth creation, a seemingly contradictory conclusion for the world to reach when you have no other motivation than to gain more.

But greed is not the motive of a Prosperous Home. We are Holy-Spirit-led, grafted-in People of the Book. The Bible is clear that giving is our spiritual responsibility for the sake of others and ourselves. Looking back to ancient Israel, their giving system supported all public and private welfare needs. There was no federal program to rely upon for help—no separation of church and state as we Americans have grown to expect. Instead, the only way for Israel's poor to survive was through the mandatory generosity of the average giver. This grass-roots involvement was God's idea for the prevention of entitlement among His people.

In those days, giving was self-directed, meaning the givers were expected to decide themselves where they should give. Money was given directly to persons in need. Dizzying rules were created to manage the nationwide mandate, much as our tax and welfare laws do for Americans today. Again, a portion of giving, called maaser, was separated for the support of priests and synagogues and schools teaching the Torah—which became the basis for the Western concept of the tithe. Giving was intended for citizens and aliens alike, flowing from the strength of people as they became aware of needs around them.

But helping the poor was not the primary reason for those ancient giving laws. According to rabbinical tradition, God's first concern was for the sake of the giver. The very root of all giving was primarily to build the character of the one who had the money, and secondarily for the benefit of the receiver. Jesus Himself echoed this historical mindset to the early church:

> *In everything I showed you that by working hard in this manner you must help the weak and remember the words of the Lord Jesus, that He Himself said, "It is more blessed to give than to receive."*
>
> *Acts 20:35b NASB*

Generosity is a priority for a Prosperous Home because Christians love giving. We love to share God's goodness through evangelism and tangible care, to demonstrate God's nature, and to make ourselves better in the process. This means LGS has a pecking order: give first, save second, and live on what remains.

Living is priority 3
Giving is priority 1
Saving is priority 2

These priorities do not compete with your Purpose Train exercise from Chapter 1. Neither are they new to revivalist thinking. Rather, these priorities converge to accomplish your purpose. Consider this quote from 1872 on the subject of priorities:[15]

"Gain all you can, save all you can, and give all you can."
"The Use of Money," Sermon 50, by John Wesley

In conclusion, my conviction on giving is simple: Cheerfully sow both tithes and offerings. Tithes go to support the storehouse, which means your home church. Offerings begin after the tithe, meaning 11% and beyond, and may be self-directed as you become aware of a need. Above all, understand that Giving and Saving are seed, and little bread will come unless you remember to sow.

From this point forward, I demonstrate LGS with a presumed tithe of 10%. This is for ease of understanding and not to communicate a law or perpetuate guilt for those who choose to give below 10%. How you sow is a personal matter, and there is much to learn through the confusion surrounding giving. For more information, read my forthcoming book, *Giver—Tithes and Offerings for the Follower of Jesus.*

---

15 *"Wesley put restrictions on the way we gain all we can. Earning money was discouraged if it came at the expense of our own health, whether physical or spiritual. This caution rules out gaining all one can through 'workaholism' or through any means that leads us to cheat, lie, or in any way violate the standards that Christians ought to hold. Nor should we earn money at the expense of another person's physical or spiritual health. The business we conduct should be fitting to a life dedicated to God.*

"Similarly, the way we save all we can also matters. Wesley's idea runs much deeper than getting a good deal or buying things on sale. What we buy matters as much as what we pay for it. For Wesley, saving meant avoiding any expense that was simply for our own pleasure, rather than for taking care of a legitimate need. He understood that indulging our desires could lead us away from God. He also understood that spending money on unnecessary items left less for us to give to others. The point of saving is not hoarding; it is giving.

"To give all we can is to reflect God's own generosity and thus to participate in God's work. We are to manage our money and property to be able to use it for God's purposes. If we think about the use of money as a spiritual discipline, then we can see that the point is not to give away what we think is extra. The point is to play our role in distributing God's resources equitably, not denying our own needs, but seeing the needs of others to be as legitimate as our own." Excerpt from A Year with John Wesley and Our Methodist Values, by F. Douglas Powe, Jr., Henry H. Knight, III, Michael J. Coyner, Randy L. Maddox, and Sarah Heaner Lancaster, p. 48.

SAVING

As I mentioned earlier, the word Saving is a misnomer, but it is a simple way to illustrate how net worth is captured from income. Really, Saving is anything that flows from the bottom of your funnel onto the balance sheet. It can either increase assets or decrease debts—both drive net worth higher.

Rising net worth has the obvious benefit of acting as a bumper around your home to protect when unknown but foreseeable problems arise. Net worth represents a cushion of time in the event some or all of your income streams slow or stop. Rising net worth has the added reward of making yourself into a bank, meaning you break the debt cycle of borrowing and interest expense whenever you can absorb the impact of difficulties yourself without using credit or borrowing. But there is one more important benefit of rising net worth, one that I believe has been lost to American homes: financial vitality.

When I say vitality, I mean the capacity to endure and build a home that is secure and resilient to harm. America is a great nation. Our citizens enjoy the purest water, the finest medical and legal services, and even our schools are second to none. But in all this blessing, many homes live vulnerable in their financial condition. Easy borrowing and constant comfort have engendered a moral hazard of entitlement for many Americans.

The New Oxford American Dictionary defines vitality as "the state of being strong and active." Early Americans understood financial vitality. I'm thinking of the farmers, inventors, and builders who made this great nation. Times were harsh, and families depended on God and others for their survival. The Jews understand this even more, their people having suffered terrible assaults. As a result, they think and live with a mind towards financial vitality.

I have been studying ancient Israel and Jewish culture for many years. One of the most surprising discoveries has been the almost cellular bias they carry for financial vitality. Some accuse them of greed, but I see this as an execution of purpose. They are a people of great financial capacity, who live a rich tradition designed to protect and perpetuate their culture and those who harbor among them.

Studying rabbinical laws on giving revealed this surprising application of financial vitality: A good Jew's maximum giving each year, with very limited exceptions, was not to exceed 20%. The reason for this limit was to prevent a giver from falling into need. The Jews had a formal tradition of building wealth for the sake of other Jews in distress. Remember their self-directed giving? Partly, that was so givers could help family and friends recover from poverty. In fact, tithes would not be expected of a good Jew until the person or newly married couple reached and exceeded a minimum financial level of self-sustainability. While even the homeless were expected to make offerings, tithes were delayed until the home became sustainable. This is the exact opposite to what I see taught about giving in American churches. Some pastors encourage tithing to their church even if the gift destabilizes the home. My point is not to blame or argue, but rather to encourage the historic virtue of stability in a home. Financial vitality is part of a Prosperous Home tradition and strategy. I believe this because it is part of our early church tradition, as described here by our esteemed apostle Paul:

> *But if anyone does not provide for his own, and especially for those of his household, he has denied the faith and is worse than an unbeliever.*
>
> *1 Timothy 5:8 NASB*

The Saving category of LGS establishes a higher priority to raising net worth than you may have ever understood to be proper for a Christian. This priority is not about greed or entitlement or selfish ambition. Rather, it is founded on the idea of generosity from a place of strength rather than weakness.

As Christians, we are each called to help others. According to the apostle James, God sees this done best by aiding orphans and widows, and by keeping ourselves unstained by the world. This type of living can be done with or without wealth; it matters not to God, for the heart test is the same either way. We can do little or much, but wealth determines how far we will reach because, as I've said earlier, Money is a spiritual power. And power always exaggerates whatever is in our heart. With a pure heart, and much wealth, we can accomplish far more than in any other combination of that formula. May God bless your Giving, Giving, and Saving all for the glory of Christ's will:

> *And this I pray, that your love may abound still more and more in real knowledge and all discernment, so that you may approve the things that are excellent, in order to be sincere and blameless until the day of Christ; having been filled with the fruit of righteousness which comes through Jesus Christ, to the glory and praise of God.*
>
> *Philippians 1:9-11 NASB*

LESSONS

CHAPTER SEVEN

HOMEWORK

Complete the LGS Practice Sheet on the next page.

VIDEO

Watch video #7 entitled, "Saving Changes the Balance Sheet," on your DVD or online curriculum.

Watch tutorial video #8 entitled, "Kinds of Seed," on your DVD or online curriculum.

GOING DEEPER

What is the purpose of Giving and Saving?

What is your view on giving?

Why is Giving and Saving considered "seed"?

Is the tithe relevant today?

Is saving important to you?

What are your views on being wealthy? Is it good or bad to be wealthy?

What are your thoughts on giving not exceeding 20%?

FURTHER STUDY

Read or memorize these verses: Malachi 3:10-12, Luke 19:17, 1 Timothy 5:8, Philippians 1:9-11.

Download and read a copy of "The Use of Money," Sermon 50, by John Wesley.

Make a $10 donation to a charitable cause of your choice.

Match your Giving with equal Saving for one month.

Open a savings account if you have not done so already.

PRAYER

Father God, thank You for Your heart of generosity towards us. Thank You that we get to participate in that generosity. Show us Your heart for where to sow seed, and wisdom for how to establish stability and growth in our home.

PROPHETIC ACT

Do your homework for this chapter.

LGS
PRACTICE SHEET

If a person has monthly income of:	And an LGS of:	Calculate the: *(answers on pg.226)*
$1,000	90/10/0	Monthly Savings: ________
$4,123	80/10/10	Monthly Living: ________
$2,444	93/3/4	Monthly Giving: ________
$9,999	70/15/15	Annual Saving: ________
$1,901,000	10/57/33	Semi-annual Living:________
$1000	90/10/0	Annual Giving: ________

If a person's income is $4,000, and she gives $500 and saves $600, what is she likely spending on living?

If a person is living on $3,000, giving $600, and saving $500, but added new debt of $200, what is her income?

If a person is living on 83%, giving 13% and saving 6%, but adds new debt of 2%, what is her saving percentage?

If a person's giving is 13%, how much is his offering percentage?

If a person is living on 102%, how much is his saving percentage?

If a person is living on 100%, how much is his seed?

If a person's combined giving and saving percentage is 30%, how much is his living percentage?

If a person's tithe equals $300, how much is his total income?

NOTES

CHAPTER 08

READY, AIM, TEST

We have covered much ground over the last seven chapters. Let's make a quick review of what we've covered. Chapters 1 and 2 focused on the spiritual power of money and how to align our money behind our purpose. Chapters 3 and 4 focused on the balance sheet equation and how net worth is carried. Chapter 5 introduced the cash flow equation and the three types of income. Chapters 6 and 7 complete the income equation as a funnel and how all spending is captured in the tool I call LGS (Living, Giving, and Savings). Now it is time to propose an effective plan for growing your wealth.

In Chapter 4, we had our first opportunity to make a target. We built a Target Balance Sheet projected one year from today. The exercise was detailed enough to target future assets and debts line by line. But the target still needs a sound strategy in order to achieve it.

Many people dream and declare proclamations for the future. All of them are backed by enthusiasm and hope, but very few are supported by a plan to actually arrive at the goal. Financial dreams are similar, except they have one major advantage: the plan can be tested. We've learned two key equations and the LGS tool. Using these like building blocks, we can see whether a plan exists and if it is rigorous enough to accomplish the dream.

Net Worth = Asset – Deb; **Inflows** = Outflows;
Income = Living + Giving + Saving

Refer back to Chapter 4, where you completed a one-year Target Balance Sheet exercise. Go there now and review the details of that exercise. I've brought the totals from the bottom of that exercise here for easy reference:

	TODAY'S BALANCE SHEET	TARGET AFTER 1 YEAR	CHANGES BY LINE
NET WORTH	$51,675	$59,500	$7,825

You will recall that Column 1 is today's net worth, which was derived by the balance sheet equation subtracting debts from assets as of "today." Column 2 is the targeted net worth, again derived as assets minus debts, except the values are derived as an intelligent guess about one year from now. Column 3 is the change for every line, taking into account all the line targets for the coming year. The Column 3 total of $7,825 represents the targeted change for the year, viewed from the balance sheet perspective. Now the question before us is whether our LGS plan supports the targeted change? And if not, how can we adjust so our plan achieves our target?

MAKING A PLAN

The LGS tool says that spending for Living and Giving has no effect upon the balance sheet. Therefore, the only way to reach the target is through the Saving category. For example, if you have an LGS of 80/10/10 and your total spending is $5,000 per month, your LGS plan in dollars would look like this.

L	$4,000	80% (80% x monthly spending of $5,000)
G	$500	10% (10% x monthly spending of $5,000)
S	$500	10% (10% x monthly spending of $5,000)
Total	$5,000	100%

The LGS we used above was a monthly figure, so one year from now, our plan is to set aside twelve deposits of $500 for an annualized LGS Savings of $6,000. Comparing that to our Column 3 target reveals that our plan doesn't quite support our Target Balance Sheet changes of $7,825.

Now, we have two clear perspectives of the same goal for growing net worth. Either can be groomed to accomplish the goal. In this example, the person can adjust her LGS to put more toward Savings. An LGS of 77/10/13 would do it. Can you see how?[16] Or this person can go back to the drawing board and revise her Target Balance Sheet lines using smarter information. Probably, this person will adjust the balance sheet to match LGS and reduce Column 2 targets down to equal the LGS annual saving of $6,000. Regardless of how one chooses, the Column 3 total and the annualized LGS savings should be the same amounts.

16 *Target balance sheet change of $7,825 divided by annualized income $60,000 ($5,000 x 12 months) equals .1304, or 13%. If she chooses to maintain her tithe, the higher savings must come entirely from the Living category. Therefore, the new LGS would need to be 77/10/13. This is very doable, but most families need time to work their Living percentage lower and make room for higher Giving and Savings.*

Below, I have adjusted the original example to compliment the LGS annual Saving of $6,000. I chose to build assets over debt reductions. People's approach can be different depending on their individual convictions and circumstances. Line-by-line revisions are shown in bold to illustrate the details.

	TODAY'S BALANCE SHEET	TARGET AFTER 1 YEAR	CHANGES BY LINE
Cash on Hand	$400	$400	$0
Emergency Cash	$0	$1,000	$1,000
Savings for a New Car	$200	$1,200	$1,000
Toyota Car	$4,000	$4,000	$0
Chevy Pickup	$8,500	$8,500	$0
Jewelry	$1,000	$1,000	$0
Furniture & Antiques	$2,500	$2,500	$0
Home	$200,000	$201,000	$1,000
IRA Retirement Savings	$2,000	$2,000	$0
401k Retirement Savings	$900	$1,900	$1,000
TOTAL ASSETS	**$219,500**	**$223,500**	**$4,000**
Chase Credit Card	**$1,900**	**$1,825**	**-$75**
VISA Credit Card	$3,900	$3,800	-$100
MasterCard	$425	$0	-$425
Toyota Car Loan	$4,500	$4,300	-$200
Chevy Pickup Loan	$8,100	$7,900	-$200
Home Mortgage	$149,000	$148,000	-$1,000
TOTAL DEBTS	**$167,825**	**$165,825**	**-$2,000**
NET WORTH	**$51,675**	**$57,675**	**$6,000**

Notice how the Column 3 total of $6,000 equals the LGS annual Savings of $6,000. This demonstrates convergence of a Target Balance Sheet and an LGS plan. The plan is sound and there is little doubt that this family will reach their financial dreams and declarations. And even in the storms of unwelcome income dips and spending spikes, this family will reach its goal with the great advantage of aim, perseverance, and, of course, God.

Saving 10% = $500 (10% x monthly spending of $5,000) x 12 months = $6,000

LGS DETAIL WORKSHEET

Often LGS planning is something that evolves. When I first began using the LGS tool, I needed to see where I currently was. You may need to do this as well. Using the spaces below, record your initial Target Balance Sheet totals and compare that to your current LGS. Problems with your plan will quickly become apparent. Refine your plan using the steps above until you land on a sound LGS plan that will support your refined balance sheet targets.

	TODAY'S BALANCE SHEET	TARGET AFTER 1 YEAR	CHANGES BY LINE
NET WORTH			

Current Monthly LGS (as % and $)			Planned Monthly LGS (as % and $)		
L	______%	$______	L	______%	$______
G	______%	$______	G	______%	$______
S	______%	$______	S	______%	$______
Total	______%	$______	Total	______%	$______

Multiplying the monthly LGS Savings times 12 will render an LGS annual Savings. Continue to pray and refine until your LGS annualized savings is equal to Column 3 above. If you need further help, see video exercise or seek help from a Prosperous Soul coach.

Once you have an LGS plan that supports the Target Balance Sheet, you can back into the gritty details of an LGS Master Sheet. That work happens on a large worksheet (called the LGS Master Sheet) where you are the master and money is your servant. This is where each category of LGS is broken down into specific groups.

Living	Giving	Saving
Housing	Tithe	Adding Assets
Auto	Offering	Reducing Debts
Personal	Other Giving	
Medical		
Education		
Entertainment		
Taxes & Office		

Most financial courses work from details like these up into a grand monthly budget, but I prefer working backwards from an LGS plan. My approach tells you what you are allocating to Living, Giving, and Saving from a Purpose Train perspective rather than allowing your spending habits and commitments to rule your decisions. It is a practical application of happening to your life rather than life happening to you.

Because most of us wrestle with spending in the moment, like at the grocery checkout or tire store counter, we should already have some idea of how much goes where at a detail level. A sample LGS Master Sheet is available at the end of this chapter. Soon, I hope to create a powerful and convenient smartphone application to make this work even easier and more powerful.

To complete the LGS Master Sheet, take your Planned LGS in dollars and place them on the total lines for Living, Giving, and Spending. This is the planned maximum for each major category. Now go through the work of spreading each total over the known and expected categories under each group.

The Giving group will be easy. Simply take the planned giving in dollars and spread it across either the tithe and/or offering lines according to your giving plan. Sum your planned tithe and offering lines to prove it matches your giving plan total.

The Saving group will also be easy. Simply take the planned saving in dollars and place it into either the asset increases or debt decreases lines you already planned on your Target Balance Sheet. The hard work you've already done on the Target Balance Sheet makes this work fast and easy. Cross-check the total savings with your Column 3 targeted change.

The Living group will require more work, but it too should prove simple. Take the planned living in dollars and place it on the appropriate total line for the Living category. Now, complete as many known categories as you can. For example, rent and utilities can be accurately entered from memory. Also, set your grocery budget from experience. Line by line, move through the living group until you have all the lines your lifestyle requires. Sum the lines to test your total. If you have more dollars on lines than the plan's total allows, reduce lines where you can. Continue to groom your living lines until the sum equals the plan. This can take several attempts if you are building a tight plan for the first time. This process gets much easier as months roll past, so don't stop until your plan is stretched across all the groups under Living, Giving, and Saving. If you need further help, I suggest seeking help from a Prosperous Soul coach.

LESSONS

CHAPTER EIGHT

HOMEWORK

Build your LGS Master Sheet found on pages 116-119.

VIDEO

Watch video #8 entitled, "Ready, Aim, Test," on your DVD or online curriculum.

Watch tutorial video #9 entitled, "LGS Plan," on your DVD or online curriculum.

GOING DEEPER

What difficulties or relief came up while building your LGS Master Sheet and refining your Target Balance Sheet?

How was it different building your LGS Master Sheet from your LGS versus figuring out your LGS from your "needs"?

What surprises or new revelation came up while you filled in the actual numbers for your LGS Master Sheet?

What goals did you have to change to balance your Target Balance Sheet?

Do you or have you in the past rebelled from a budget? If so, why?

What ways have you used in the past to help you stay on budget?

How will building your budget from an LGS that is in line with your Purpose Train change your ability or desire to follow your budget?

FURTHER STUDY

Complete a Target Balance Sheet and identify your annual net change (Column 3).

Complete an LGS Plan and identify your annual savings plan.

Refine your Target Balance Sheet or LGS Plan until the target change (Column 3) equals your annualized Savings from your LGS Plan.

PRAYER

Father God, thank You for being my provider. Help me always to remember that. Thank You for meeting all of my financial needs and growing me into being a powerful person in my finances, filled with purpose and intentionality.

PROPHETIC ACT

Declare over your life this week, "GOD IS MY PROVIDER."

LGS

MASTER SHEET

	Current	%	Yr 1 Target	%	Yr 2 Target	%	Yr 3 Target	%
INCOME								
Wages & Tips-net								
Interest & Dividends								
Child Support & Alimony								
Gifts/Honoraria Received								
Known Bonus								
Transfer From Savings								
Retirement								
Other								
Other								
TOTAL								
LIVING- HOUSING EXPENSES								
Mortgage/Rent*								
Home/Rental Insurance								
Electricity/Gas/Oil								
Water/Sewer/Trash								
Phone								
Cable/Satellite								
Internet								
Furnishings & Appliances								
Lawn & Garden								
Maintenance & Supplies								
Improvements								
Other								
TOTAL								

	Current	%	Yr 1 Target	%	Yr 2 Target	%	Yr 3 Target	%
LIVING- AUTO EXPENSES								
Car Payments*								
Fuel								
Bus/Taxi/Train Fare								
Repairs								
Registration/License								
Auto Insurance								
TOTAL								
LIVING- PERSONAL EXPENSES								
Groceries								
Dining & Eating Out								
Personal Supplies								
Cleaning, Clothing, & Hair								
Pets								
Other								
TOTAL								
LIVING- HEALTH EXPENSES								
Health Insurance								
Doctor & Dentist								
Medicine & Drugs								
Health Club Dues								
Life Insurance								
Other								
TOTAL								
LIVING- ENTERTAINMENT EXPENSES								
Movies & Music								
Games & Books								
Events & Holidays								
Sports & Hobbies								
Other								
TOTAL								

	Current	%	Yr 1 Target	%	Yr 2 Target	%	Yr 3 Target	%
LIVING- EDUCATION EXPENSE								
Newspaper & Magazines								
Dues & Memberships								
Child Education (All fees)								
Adult Education (All fees)								
Other								
TOTAL								
LIVING- ADMIN & TAX EXPENSE								
Student Loan Minimum*								
Credit Card Minimum*								
Bank Fees & Postage								
Child Support & Alimony								
Taxes								
Other								
TOTAL								
GIVING								
Pledges Paid								
Charitable Donations								
Offerings and Gifts								
Tithe								
TOTAL								
SAVINGS								
Emergency Fund								
Transfer to Savings								
Retirement (401k, IRA)								
Investments								
Education								
Vacation/Travel								
Other								
TOTAL								

	Current	%	Yr 1 Target	%	Yr 2 Target	%	Yr 3 Target	%
DEBT**								
Home Mortgage								
Auto Loan								
Student Loan								
Credit Card Debt								
Other								
TOTAL								
TOTAL INCOME								
TOTAL LIVING								
TOTAL GIVING								
TOTAL SAVING								
TOTAL DEBT								
TOTAL EXPENSES								
SHORTFALL/SURPLUS								

NOTES

CHAPTER 09

BALANCING YOUR LIFESTYLE

In Chapter 6, I wrote about living within your means. Everyone understands the wisdom of preserving the balance between income and spending. But what happens when spending is greater? What happens when living costs are simply higher than earnings? How does a Prosperous Home approach challenges like these?

Spending more than income is like a ship taking on water. It can happen in small amounts and for short seasons, but cannot be ignored for long, or considered acceptable except in bursts and under careful stewardship. When a home spends more than its income, savings should be used as a bridge rather than borrowing. Easy borrowing becomes a great temptation because debt is a convenient painkiller. It enables people to solve urgency with haste, postponing what may be the difficult but important step of balancing your lifestyle.

It's obvious that everyone experiences financial storms in life. Sometimes those storms strike quickly. Unwelcome events like lost jobs or major repairs should be tackled quickly and decisively, like an emergency. Explore every option and respond when appropriate. For example:

- Respond intentionally and with full understanding. Never react in haste.
- Remember to pray for God's intervention. Don't pray in fear like an orphan, but as an adopted child.

- Consider making a sacrificial offering. It need not be large, but it must be cheerful.
- Seek replacement employment, start a home business, or find temporary side jobs.
- Investigate unemployment and other social benefits to bridge the season.
- Reject stigma and guilt. Don't use the enemy's weapons on yourself.
- Weigh the need to downsize. Take steps to preserve the vitality of your home.

Some readers may wonder, "Where's the faith in that?" I would answer, in all of it. Steps like these are done in faith because we understand that God is our provider. And, yes, He sometimes provides through government assistance. In ancient Israel, the giving laws (Tzadakah) were simply that: God's welfare system over a nation. In America, our system relies on taxes and government programs to provide the bulk of welfare care. I don't mean to imply we have it right; actually, I feel our system demonstrates an absenteeism in the Church's cultural role. But that is the subject of another book and I believe God is behind every good thing governmental programs might offer. Forsaking these benefits without full understanding is to avail oneself of only a portion in God's provision.

I'm reminded of the story of a terrible flood. The water rose until the homeowner was forced to retreat to his rooftop. He prayed for God to deliver, so God sent a raft. The homeowner refused to float away and continued praying. Next, God sent a rowboat with men aboard. Again, the man sent them away, saying he was waiting for God to deliver. Finally, a helicopter flew by and lowered a rope. The man waved it off and continued praying for deliverance. The water continued its rise until the homeowner perished. In heaven, the man asked God why he had not been rescued, to which God responded, "Son, I tried three times. I am able to use everything practical and miraculous. It is all under My control."

> *To the pure, all things are pure; but to those who are defiled and unbelieving, nothing is pure, but both their mind and their conscience are defiled.*
>
> *Titus 1:15 NASB*

> *All things are lawful for me, but not all things are profitable. All things are lawful for me, but I will not be mastered by anything.*
>
> *1 Corinthians 6:12 NASB*

Investigate every option when navigating a sudden storm. I offer the truism, good sailors are not made on flat seas. Understand that storms are teaching moments, and learn all you can in difficult times. As well as you are able, take actions that follow your Purpose Train. Review and refine your identity and purpose wording, take supporting actions, and do them in faith, not fear. Resist the temptation to ignore the important things you should be doing while you respond to urgent circumstances.

PLANS FOR IMBALANCE

There are times when a Prosperous Home plans for spending to exceed income. One example is education. A full-time student may need to postpone working while he or she completes a college or university degree. Income may cease while living costs continue, but this imbalance is done with care and stewardship. The timeline is controlled and net worth is protected as much as possible.

Another example of plans for imbalance happen during the start-up or expansion phase of a company. Imbalance is always risky, but risk isn't evil. Life requires risk. Succeed in these seasons using your Purpose Train, prayer, and hard work. Seek wise counsel. Pray like you mean it. In all cases, avoid debt or use it with great respect.

> *On the day I called, You answered me; You made me bold with strength in my soul.*
>
> *Psalms 138:3 NASB*

> *Without consultation, plans are frustrated, but with many counselors they succeed.*
>
> *Proverbs 15:22 NASB*

Balance in your lifestyle happens when the majority of time your income is adequate for all ordinary Living, Giving, and Saving. Think of this lifestyle as being flexible, able to adapt to a plan, but always returning to this balance as a stewardship priority. To illustrate what I mean by flexible, think of how a compass actively provides a heading to follow, regardless of a changing location. The flexibility of the compass is similar to the idea of balancing the equation. Wherever your plans take you, return to the priority of keeping income equal to all your ordinary spending for Living, Giving, and Saving.

CHRONIC OVERSPENDING

Many American homes exist in a chronic out-of-balance condition. They are not in a season of education or expansion, but instead are simply consuming too much as a rule, and net worth is suffering.

Chronic overspending tends to sneak up on families. It begins with the pursuit of a dream but eventually paints families into a corner, with seemingly no way of escape except the death of the dream. But that feeling is rarely true, and nearly always this conflict can be resolved with a few inspired tools.

This next section offers four progressive tools known as empowered choice, potted plant syndrome, the priority war, and the financial reset. Each of these tools are described below in progressive order, meaning a family should move through a tool, and advance to the next tool only if their circumstances warrant a more aggressive approach. If you wish to apply these tools, I recommend seeking help from a professional or Prosperous Soul coach.

The first weapon is the idea of empowered choice. Choice is something we all have regardless of circumstances. We choose who we will be on the inside, and our money is an expression of who we are because it is a spiritual power that exaggerates what lies within. So, express yourself well by controlling your spending. Much trouble comes for people who have no control over their spirit; in fact, the Bible warns us away from that condition:

> *Like a city that is broken into and without walls is a man who has no control over his spirit.*
>
> *Proverbs 25:28 NASB*

Seek God's help in areas that require self control. Seek a Financial Sozo or other pastoral care if you feel this would help. Demonstrate stewardship by expressing your power to choose what spending should stop.

This idea of control was mentioned earlier in the phrase happen to life, rather than let life happen to you. Your ability to make empowered choices that restrain spending should be made in alignment with your Purpose Train. Exert your power over spending by cutting what does not support your Purpose Train. All spending that doesn't support your family's identity, purpose, vision, and strategies should be eliminated.

POTTED PLANT SYNDROME

Dawna and I have been together since 1981. I was one year past high school when she danced in my arms at her senior ball. Shortly after, we were married.

Dawna was college-bound, so I agreed to try university as well. During those early years we were young and completely uninformed about money and purpose, and we didn't know Jesus. Every month was a financial challenge. We barely paid for tuition, groceries, and rent in our tiny city apartment. This continued through college and into our early careers. It worsened when we had children and purchased a house. Raising a family and paying a mortgage proved a very steep climb for our blossoming lifestyle.

Gradually, raises and promotions came along to relieve the tight monthly battle. Yet we still held our breath most months. We marveled every year at tax time, exclaiming, "I can't believe we made that much money. Where did it all go?" This continued into our mid-thirties, until one day Dawna and I realized we had unknowingly accepted an orphan mindset that "more is always better." I called this "potted plant syndrome."

Imagine your favorite houseplant in a clay pot. Because it is new, its soil is rich, loose, and well-watered. The plant thrives in this new home. Sunlight, clean water, and warm soil cause the plant to thrive. Its roots go deep, exploring the reaches of its clay pot. Foliage spreads and flowers as the plant grows.

Months later, the plant begins to grow stressed as its clay container becomes too constraining to support its foliage. Roots grow impacted, knotting against the walls of the original pot. Water barely penetrates the soil for all its root-bound condition. The plant urgently awaits rescue. Suddenly, the plant is lifted from its small prison and relief comes.

A new, larger pot appears and its tight root ball relaxes in dark new soil. Refreshing water awakens the roots and once again the foliage grateful spreads. This cycle of desperation repeats itself, pulling the houseplant into an endless cycle of struggle, because the plant only knows one thing: more is better. Such was our early financial lives.

God is a rewarder of those who seek Him. This fact doesn't change, whether we have little or much. But our endless pursuit for more must be tempered to demonstrate supernatural stewardship. Like the plant, Dawna and I only understood stewardship to be an endless reach for more, which entirely depended upon increasing income. Our only restraint was external, imposed by our environment. Lifestyle was happening to us, rather than us happening to lifestyle. We had no emotional framework for self-restraint, except to cry out when our roots grew knotted by times of crisis.

We were generous givers in all those seasons. But our appetite for more was like that plant, managed only when our income-environment grew too limited to support our spread. We stewarded by Braille, meaning we always spent more until our environment imposed its limit. Our only restraint was our financial wall, the wall of our clay pot. In terms of LGS, I estimate we were something like 90/10/0 in those days. But God was calling us to something deeper. He suggested we decide in advance the lifestyle we wanted, to prune ourselves rather than push into the clay wall, and settle there to bear more fruit. So we did.

Dawna and I considered the home in which we lived, the cars we drove, and clothes we wore. We considered the way we ate and the schools our children attended. Every aspect was sorted according to our purpose and we made choices accordingly. We learned that a larger home was not important to our purpose. We discovered gratitude for our used autos and stopped vying for more.

This process came early for us, but turns out to be a typical pattern in older Americans. Social science calls this a consumption curve. A consumption curve graphs an individual's spending over a lifetime. Usually, consumption peaks in the mid-sixties, after children graduate, marry, and move away. The mortgage finally gets paid off and lifestyle goals move into retirement mode. Without the Purpose Train, retirees perpetuate the potted plant syndrome by living to the edges of their retirement pot. Income tends to be smaller and consumption is reduced as they concede to a smaller pot. In the end, lifestyle still happens to them rather than the more powerful mode of happening to their lifestyle.

With God's help, Dawna and I simply began reducing our peak consumption in alignment with our purpose. This wasn't easy, since many of our friends were buying new and larger homes (and many of them still are). But we were content to live simply. We chose to spend well inside the walls of our clay pot and abandon crisis as our tutor.

Imagine our delight when we learned that God had not finished repotting us. Our incomes continued to grow and multiply, and since our consumption was lower, the dollars were freed to give and save. This experience deeply affected my understanding of bread and seed, which we discussed earlier. As time moved along, we learned to manage our lives proactively and joyfully, well within the walls of whatever income we found ourselves. In retrospect, I attribute our best ideas all to God's invitation. It has helped our living quality, our marriage, and our children's relationship with money. Now, it can help you in the form of this manual. Let the potted plant syndrome lead you away from crisis as a tutor. Learn how to stop struggling against the limits of your environment and happen to life. Reduce your consumption curve early, and on purpose, and reap the rewards of God's timing.

Other teachers encourage the idea of deferred gratification. Delaying spending is a balance sheet idea that protects net worth by avoiding debt. This is a good habit, and biblical besides, but it is not the same as addressing the potted plant syndrome. Rather than merely delaying spending, you tackle the potted plant syndrome by using the Purpose Train to eliminate spending that doesn't belong in a Prosperous Home. Spending goes lower because the consumption curve is introduced earlier, not merely because you postpone spending. These two ideas working together can correct many problems in a home suffering from chronic overspending.

My hope is that your cash flow equation can be balanced with the tools of empowered choice and potted plant syndrome. In the next chapter, I explain the two remaining tools: priority war and financial reset. These two are more disruptive ways to end chronic overspending. However, implementation of these tools falls beyond the scope of this manual. If you are interested in learning more, I recommend seeking a Prosperous Soul coach or professional adviser. Again, hopefully those tools are not required. To that end, allow me to pray for you and your home now, that you can take flight as a supernatural steward, easily and under God's grace for change.

> *Father in heaven, You are holy and forgiving. You know every detail of this home; nothing is hidden from Your eyes. You have good plans and You are invited to inhabit this home with Your great riches. Wisdom and love, hope and courage, faith and obedience—all the virtues of Your kingdom—come upon this steward and this home.*
>
> *You value our needs and wants, and this person is a child whom You love. I request Your good rescue now. I summon Your gentle encouragement. I anticipate Your empowered choices being revealed. God bless this steward, and God bless this Prosperous Home.*

LESSONS
CHAPTER NINE

HOMEWORK

Invite a trustworthy friend or coach to review your Balance Sheet and Cash Flow Equation. Explain how your LGS spending aligns with your Purpose Train. Ask not to convince, but to invite constructive feedback.

VIDEO

Watch video #9 entitled, "Balancing Your Lifestyle," on your DVD or online curriculum.

Watch tutorial video #10 entitled, "The Potted Plant Syndrome" on your DVD or online curriculum.

Watch tutorial video #11 entitled, "Making an LGS Plan" on your DVD or online curriculum.

GOING DEEPER

How does comparing your needs versus wants affect your stress level?

What have you done in the past to address being out of balance in your finances?

What pruning is God inviting you into to curb your spending habits?

Knowing that using debt to spend can delay consequences for a time, what is one way you can help balance your lifestyle today?

What is an adequate amount of money for your emergency fund that can act as a buffer for emergencies you might face?

Looking back on your budget sheet, are there areas you can cut that don't support your Purpose Train?

FURTHER STUDY

Read or memorize the following verses: Psalms 138:3, Proverbs 15:22, Proverbs 25:28, 1 Corinthians 6:12, Titus 1:15.

Read Shawn Bolz's book, Keys to Heaven's Economy.

Choose a target for your efforts, whether it's building an emergency fund or paying off a certain debt. Create a timeline and a chart for tracking your progress. Share that with someone you trust.

PRAYER

Father God, thank You for Your pruning in my life. Thank You for helping me to bring purpose to my life so that I can live a balanced lifestyle that grows and bears fruit in the right way. Speak clearly to me about the areas of my life that need pruning, and give me grace to cut those pieces away.

PROPHETIC ACT

Using the prayer at the end of Chapter 9, write out a declaration over your own home. Dedicate your home to God in a simple ceremony using the declaration, and place it in a safe deposit box or time capsule for future reference.

OFFERING READING #1

BETHEL CHURCH

As we receive today's offering,
We are believing the Lord for:

Jobs and better jobs
Raises and bonuses
Benefits
Sales and commissions
Favorable settlements
Estates and inheritances

Interests and income
Rebates and returns
Checks in the mail
Gifts and surprises
Finding money
Debts paid off
Expenses decrease
Blessing and increase

Thank You, Lord,
for meeting all of my financial needs
that I may have more than enough
to give into the Kingdom of God
and promote the Gospel of
Jesus Christ.

Hallelujah!!!

NOTES

CHAPTER 10

PRIORITY
WAR & HASTE

The priority war is a powerful way to find solutions in very difficult financial storms. I reserve this tool for times when easy cuts are exhausted and deeper cuts threaten to disrupt a family's core priorities. The priority war is effective for singles or couples at any age or economic level.

Most people come to me late, after excessive spending has run a long and damaging course. Reserves are usually exhausted and debt has grown unmanageable. At this stage, discouragement and fear are common. People feel stigmatized by failure and shame, often questioning whether God is helping at all. The first thing I strongly suggest to those in this situation is a Financial Sozo, through which hope can be restored and stigma can be sent back to the enemy. Recognize that the feelings of pain and fear are real, but not truth. Truth is what we find in the Bible. Scripture assures us that God is aware and caring. He will rescue His beloved. A Financial Sozo can help you hear from God even in a storm. From there, you can build a sound recovery plan and do the rewarding work to gain back what was eliminated using the priority war.

The tool is simple. It begins by identifying a family's top priorities. Usually these can be listed in five to ten items. Next, estimate the spending associated with each priority. Draw a line to divide the list between priorities you can afford and those you cannot, with the afforded ones above the line. Finally, challenge each priority using the Purpose Train as the monitor of importance. Cause the priorities to war between one another for the right to get above the line. Ask the hard questions. Rearrange your list as priorities shift, placing the winning priorities on top, and redraw your line. I often see family priorities shift during this exercise. This is a powerful way to reach a confident "yes" for keeping hold of what income can support and a confident "no" to those that it cannot.

PRIORITY WAR EXAMPLE

One summer, two couples came to me for advice. They came separately and their appointments fell within a week of one another. None of us were aware of what God was orchestrating, and their circumstances were nearly identical.

The first couple explained that they had limited income that fell below their ordinary living expenses. Their cash flow equation had grown wildly out of balance. Their spending was not foolish or unreasonable; rather they had young children and the demands of parenting simply overwhelmed their precarious income. Previously sweet hopes of private Christian education and home ownership had grown bitter. What should they do?

I reviewed their details and applauded their hard work, but options were slim. I explained the Jewish core value for vitality and recommended this for their home. They liked the concept, so we began by building a home Purpose Train. From that perspective, I assigned each parent to prayerfully create a list of their top ten priorities from their individual perspective. They could debate and discuss, but in the end they were each to create a confidential list and bring it to share at our next meeting one week later.

A few days later, the second couple came in with the same issues. Unintentionally, I duplicated the lesson and gave them the same instructions and assignment.

The following week, the first couple returned to go over their lists. What happened surprised me. Each spouse presented their most important priorities from their perspective. The lists were similar, but in a different order. Both lists showed only five priorities, but those five were vital. We discussed the husband's list first. He explained his reasoning to his wife while I listened quietly. I asked him to divide the list with a line between what they could afford and what they could not. A shaky line appeared between numbers 3 and 4.

Next, the wife explained her list and rationale. She too drew a line and we noticed a difference between what the two hoped to keep. Using this coachable moment, we created a new and blended list for the home. Their conversation was direct but gentle, and they soon settled in agreement with quite different results than I expected.

The line separating priorities often brings clear language to what is felt but seldom articulated. It is important to practice an environment of honor and safety as these feelings are communicated.[17] *Strong emotions should always target the list and not one another. Confronting the line between priorities on the merged list orients a couple as a team rather than competitors.* The line marks a division between what will stay and what will go in order to achieve an economically vital home. A couple should rearrange and discuss as many times as needed until they have settled upon how they will protect the priorities at the top.

This coaching step is a powerful way for loud spouses to listen, and quiet spouses to be heard. Don't underestimate this tool; some of my most surprising ministry has happened in the dialogue and discovery of what each spouse separately values. A merged list may change things entirely, and that's exactly what happened.

In the end, each family used the priority war to make powerful choices in order to protect their core family purpose. Both family's blended priority lists included family time, church, owning a home, and private Christian school for their children.

The first family chose to keep their home and place their children in public schools. The money saved on private tuition would balance their cash flow equation. It was difficult, but they reached that decision in faith and confidence. They explained their choice to me and thanked me for the newfound hope they were experiencing. I encouraged their prayerful choice, and blessed them on the journey.

Days later, the second family came with their own conclusion, which was curiously 180° opposite to the first family. They chose to let their house go back to the bank. This would free the money needed to pay for tuition. Again, I encouraged their prayerful choice, and blessed them on their journey.

Many months later, I saw each family in church. Surreptitiously, I asked the first family how they were doing.

---

17 See Danny Silk, Culture of Honor: Sustaining a Supernatural Environment (Shippensburg, PA: Destiny Publishing, 2009).

"The best decision we ever made," they told me. "Peace is back in our home and we are deeply involved with our children in public school. They love it and we are above water again. In fact, we can see our way to return our youngest child to the Christian school next year. Thank you."

I celebrated with them, excused myself, and snuck across the room to the other family. To my question, they replied like the other: "Best decision we ever made. We let our house go to the bank and rented a small apartment. This gave us enough money to accomplish our main priority of keeping our children in Christian school. And if things continue this well, we might even be able to buy another house in a year or two. But we won't rush it. Now that we've tasted financial vitality, we will never plan to live from weakness again. Thank you."

I walked away so relieved, but more than that, I was amazed at how God met each family and accomplished His good will in both circumstances. God is able to make all things work together for good, and the family that cooperates with Him will find blessed days ahead. Use your own priority war if necessary. Seek help from a Prosperous Soul coach if you need help with this powerful and freeing tool. God bless your prosperous soul.

> *And we know that God causes all things to work together for good to those who love God, to those who are called according to His purpose.*
>
> *Romans 8:28 NASB*

Building from the foundation of the Purpose Train positions a couple for cooperation when difficult financial storms demand action. With the help of gentle but direct coaching, the priority war process will feel safe and empowering. Allow the priorities to battle until the clear winners appear at the top. As a coach, I've learned to lean back and watch the Holy Spirit solve seemingly impossible financial storms. I love to let the spouses behave like the experts and rise to their challenge with wisdom and faith.

HASTE

When we find ourselves in financial pain, it is natural to respond in haste. The problem with haste is it is cousin to fear and presumption. The Bible is clear about haste. Simply put: don't do it. In whatever circumstances you find yourself, don't act in haste. Make your financial choices intentionally and in the attitude of prayer. Remain aware of God's presence, and cooperate with sound counsel. And when you act, do so with peace, faith, and wisdom.

> *The plans of the diligent lead surely to advantage, but everyone who is hasty comes surely to poverty.*
>
> *Proverbs 21:5 NASB*

> *A faithful man will abound with blessings, but he who makes haste to be rich will not go unpunished.*
>
> *Proverbs 28:20 NASB*

Lifestyle adjustments should be made slowly and strategically. Here is some good news: When adjustments require big sacrifice, they usually return to you in later days. When those sacrifices do return, it will be on your terms and God's timing. It's always better to happen to life and create a lifestyle in alignment with purpose. Make a plan to regain what you've surrendered, but always in the right timing and submission to the Holy Spirit.

> *Cast your bread on the surface of the waters, for you will find it after many days.*
>
> *Ecclesiastes 11:1 NASB*

FINANCIAL RESET

This section offers a fresh perspective on the issues surrounding the collapse of a home's economy. This includes defaults on loans, bankruptcy, and more. A financial reset is always an emotional and complex matter, best handled in peace and transparency. The subject deserves far more attention than this basic manual can offer. However, I can introduce a three-step method to begin a healing for homes facing financial troubles of this magnitude. Sound information makes for sound decisions, yet so little is written on this subject that families often drown in a vacuum of knowledge. Making matters worse, many Christians accept this vacuum because of shame or embarrassment. Emotions like these are normal, but not biblical. Ignorance is always a mistake because good stewardship requires a full understanding to navigate wisely and in biblical ways. No one feels joy when confronting the possibility of a financial collapse. Emotions and facts blur without truth, so let's bring a biblical perspective to this delicate subject.

First, if you don't need this information, spend a moment to express your gratitude before God, and then pray for mercy on those who do have the need. Ask for God to bind every effort of the enemy in their lives, and for their problems to forever "come to pass." Release Christ's hope and promise over yourself and them.

> *And the LORD gave them rest on every side, according to all that He had sworn to their fathers, and no one of all their enemies stood before them; the LORD gave all their enemies into their hand. Not one of the good promises which the LORD had made to the house of Israel failed; all came to pass.*
>
> *Joshua 21:44-45 NASB*

If you do need this information, take a deep breath and remember that God is on His throne. He knows your needs better than you do, and He will respond. Close your eyes and receive those prayers above from myself and your brothers and sisters in Christ around you. You are not forgotten or beyond Christ's ability to rescue.

Second, find your place on two scales of financial security. When some families face financial catastrophe, comparing these scales can reveal unnecessary struggles. Using your first reaction, mark your position on the measures below. On a scale of 1-10, with 1 being financial security and 10 being complete and utter financial ruin, mark the position of where your emotions say you are.

1---------2-------3------4------5------6------7------8------9------10

Now do the same exercise, using a rational mind. Remember that emotions are neither fact nor truth, but they are real. If a difference exists, we may discover evidence of emotional self-denial (on the low side) or self-condemnation (on the high side). The goal here is to land the same number on both scales. So be honest. On a scale of 1-10, with 1 being financial security and 10 being complete and utter financial ruin, mark the actual position of your financial condition.

1---------2-------3------4------5------6------7------8------9------10

If the emotional scale is different than the rational scale, I suggest a prayer of repentance and forgiveness of yourself or any others. Accept your forgiveness as a follower of Jesus and move on. If you need more help, seek a Financial Sozo. These differences are normal, but not helpful. Let's remove an unnecessary self-inflicted wound, so you can focus completely on repairing the actual financial problem.

Third, fortify your rational scale with deeper knowledge. Here are six simple definitions you need to carry in your toolbox: mortgage, collateral, insolvency, repossession, foreclosure, and bankruptcy.

Mortgage	A loan to buy land, houses, or buildings.
Collateral	Something pledged to protect the lender in case the borrower is unable to pay the debt they owe.
Insolvency	When a person is unable to pay all the debts they owe.
Repossession	When a lender takes back collateral.
Foreclosure	The repossession of mortgaged property as a result of the mortgage or's failure to keep up mortgage payments.
Bankruptcy	The legal process between borrowers and lenders when a person cannot repay the debts they owe.

Each of these definitions represents a proper and orderly process for resolving financial disasters. They are written under the rule of law, which celebrates legal process above anarchy. Without the rule of law, civilizations devolve into tribalism and violence. Rule of law is a triumph of the Holy Spirit's influence over a nation.

Here is my point: these words are not moral statements. They merely represent the legal bookends to the 10-mark of the financial security scale. They are the tools for citizens who wish to get past financial ruin and move on with their lives. Without them, a home may be destined to languish long beyond its proper time.

No financial problem is greater than these definitions, unless the problem becomes spiritual. By spiritual, I mean a condition where someone permits a Tactic to attain the level of identity or purpose. Remember your Purpose Train? Make sure your Tactics remain low, at the bottom, pulled behind the greater things of Identity, Purpose, Vision, and Strategy.

The definitions above are Tactical and nothing more. If you find yourself at a 10-mark, investigate every tool available. Don't abandon appropriate remedies on the basis of ignorance or fear. Seek knowledge and competent professional help, then ask the Lord for wisdom. Follow what He says without hesitation, and in accountability to others. You can weather this storm, and in whatever way you do, execute it in ferocious faith. God bless your Prosperous Home.

> *And without faith it is impossible to please Him, for he who comes to God must believe that He is and that He is a rewarder of those who seek Him.*
>
> *Hebrews 11:6 NASB*

LESSONS
CHAPTER TEN

HOMEWORK

Create your own Priority War Worksheet. If you are married, create a blended Priority War Worksheet with your spouse (See page 147).

VIDEO

Watch video #10 entitled, "Priority War and Haste," on your DVD or online curriculum.

Watch tutorial video #12 entitled, "Priority War," on your DVD or online curriculum.

GOING DEEPER

How has haste affected your life?

What pains or relief came up while creating your priority list?

How does creating a blended priority list affect your life and your goals?

In refocusing strong emotions toward what is possible versus against each other, how did creating a priority list help you and your spouse work through difficult financial questions?

How did using the priority war help reveal your heart or your spouse's heart?

Spend 10 minutes in prayer seeking God's heart for your finances and life. How does this revelation help you avoid haste and move forward with purpose?

FURTHER STUDY

Read or memorize the following verses: Joshua 21:44-45, Proverbs 21:5, Ecclesiastes 11:1, Romans 8:28, Hebrews 11:6.

Use a search engine to find Christian articles on these key words: mortgage, collateral, insolvency, repossession, foreclosure, and bankruptcy.

Read all or just relevant sections from Randy Alcorn's book, Money, Possessions, and Eternity.

Schedule a Financial Sozo if your emotional financial condition scale is materially different from your rational financial condition scale.

PRAYER

Holy Spirit, thank You for Your guidance as I discover the priorities in my life and my family's life. Give me grace to stick to my plan and not sabotage things when life gets hard. Thank You for Your peace as You lead us into truth and abundant life.

PROPHETIC ACT

For couples, find one way this week to show your spouse love that is not something you would typically do. If you are not married, spend twenty minutes in solitude with no phones or distractions and feel the peace of God, knowing He is working on your behalf.

PRIORITY WAR
WORKSHEET

Rank from most to least important. List more than three but no more than 10. Create your lists separately first, then present them and engineer the blend. Draw a horizontal line between the priorities where your money runs short.

	Husband List	Wife List	Blended List
1.			
2.			
3.			
4.			
5.			
6.			
7.			
8.			
9.			
10.			

NOTES

CHAPTER 11

OUTSMARTING THE BALANCE SHEET

Let's return to the cardinal fact that wise people manage wealth from the balance sheet. This is how the wealthy steward, and you can too. Learn how to increase net worth by managing assets and debts wisely into an ever-strengthening position.

The practice of outsmarting your balance sheet will never end. It is an ongoing effort, ever changing with the ebbs and flows of life. What was a prudent buy last year may be in jeopardy now. Each month, the environment will change, as well as consumer confidence and government engineering. This dynamic tide makes our job as stewards a lifetime occupation. We never retire from our assignment of sound stewardship until we arrive at those pearl gates of Revelation 21.

Although our job is continuous, I do believe we can create and maintain a perfect balance sheet. But perfection needs to be explained. The idea of perfection in most people's mind means flawless or without blemish. This definition of perfection is Greek in origin. The Hebrews thought differently. For them, perfection meant to function as designed. Their idea of perfection was one of function and purpose, not the absence of flaws. A perfect balance sheet in the Hebrew mind would be one of function and purpose. Review your Purpose Train and consider how you can express your identity and purpose through a functional and purposeful balance sheet.

There is probably much to do from now until your balance sheet achieves the Hebrew idea of perfection. We have seen the way to grow net worth through the LGS Savings.

Now let's talk about the other way to increase net worth—outsmarting your balance sheet through the prudent conversion of cash.

A balance sheet always begins with cash. Every other asset is simply a more or less prudent conversion of that cash into other forms we collectively call assets. Cash is simple to understand and easy to hold, but holding large amounts of cash over a long period leaks value. Cash evaporates like water because of inflation. This evaporation, or shrinkage, serves as a workable definition of inflation—the slight shrinkage in buying power each dollar has with the passage of time.

A simple proof of shrinkage is seen in costs across generations. Today, a movie costs around $8. When I was a boy, the price was $2. My father lamented the days of a fifty-cent show. One might think the increase is due to nicer buildings, air conditioning, and comfortable chairs. But really the price increase is caused by inflation, which means our dollar is shrinking over time, so it takes more dollars to purchase the same thing years later. My example represents approximately 70 years. Based on the U.S. Bureau of Labor Statistics (bls.gov), inflation over this same period equaled 1,322%, or approximately 18% a year (troubling in light of continual news that inflation is below 3%). Virtually all the increase in the price of movies is due to inflation over the past 70 years.

Now consider your balance sheet. Imagine you have been careful to pay off all debt and build an abundant pile of cash. Holding only cash, your net worth will likely be invested in a bank or money market fund. Those low-risk[18] cash savings tend to offer interest rates between zero and 1%. That means your cash will grow significantly slower than the average inflation over 70 years. As a young man, I didn't see this as a problem because I was headstrong and had plenty of income. Then one day it dawned on me—70 years is coming whether I'm ready or not. And at age 70, I hope to have my money working for me rather than me working for money.

That was the moment the importance of outsmarting my balance sheet became real. I would need to convert cash into smarter assets that could outrun inflation. Some assets would need to grow; others would need to go. How much cash should I hold? Should I invest in the stock market or real estate? Should I use debt as leverage to get into larger investments? And my most fundamental question of all: is it right for a Christian to accumulate assets in the first place?

---

18 *Low risk is a relative concept. I use bank savings as a common example. Savers experience lower risk due of FDIC insurance, which insures savings to a maximum limit in the case of a bank failure. Banks do fail. There are no true zero-risk investments.*

Some Christians struggle over whether money is good or evil. That internal conflict causes a spiritual dissonance that must be resolved if you plan to carry wealth. If a person fundamentally believes that money is evil, he will subconsciously avoid it, waste it, and separate himself from it. Whether we do it consciously or unconsciously, we will create or invite scenarios into our lives that siphon money away in order to be good. God has wired mankind to avoid things it perceives as a threat. Ask the Holy Spirit, "What do I really believe about money?" Get a Financial Sozo if you learn you are believing something that isn't biblically true.

The beliefs you carry in your heart are fundamental to stewardship and you must decide what is true with God's help. I am not here to convince you one way or the other. I only present this thought: live true and honest to what God is saying. Don't tolerate an unsettled heart on the matter of money. Find where your faith rests and serve God from that place. I believe money is a tool that exaggerates what we believe, so we must work hard to remove every lie and replace it with truth. Whatever your assignment with money, settle the matter until money can exaggerate your heart for Jesus, and bring His kingdom come.

CRISIS-BASED FAITH

Many people move through life like a bumper car, crashing from crisis to crisis, and calling it faith. Crisis rallies faith and dependence upon God, that much is true, and few things get our attention quicker than a thorny problem. But crisis is a cruel teacher, and there is little a person can carry or accumulate when stewarding their home like a bumper car.

It's common to express a devotion to Christ when times are hard. The mark of a Prosperous Home is to express that devotion always, especially when times are prospering. As we mature in Christ, we learn to follow the Holy Spirit in all seasons, not just those we perceive to be trials.

Learning how to stay close to God while increase happens is an ancient thread that bridges us to our believing ancestors. The Jews knew God to speak through promise and warning (see Deuteronomy 8). Today the Christian has a better covenant of grace, yet the test remains. The Book of Hebrews calls this solid food and it applies to every area of our lives, but especially money. Read this verse thoughtfully, with the eyes of a steward over money:

> *For though by this time you ought to be teachers, you have need again for someone to teach you the elementary principles of the oracles of God, and you have come to need milk and not solid food. For everyone who partakes only of milk is not accustomed to the word of righteousness, for he is an infant. But solid food is for the mature, who because of practice have their senses trained to discern good and evil.*
>
> *Hebrews 5:12-14 NASB*

Faith and dependence are minimum requirements for the poor and rich alike. I know believers who hurl themselves into continual financial disasters in order to protect a sense of dependence upon God. Sadly, this practice is more common that you may think, perpetuating a theology of weakness and financial need. The gospel of Jesus Christ is about reconciliation and restoration, and that includes our money. Imagine a shift from weakness to abundance, and how differently love is expressed through a person resolved in their relationship to money. It is an important step in spiritual maturity and I address it thoroughly through the Prosperous Soul materials. You can find these resources and more at www.prosperoussoul.com.

TREASURE OF TIME

Imagine a worker who is paid by the hour. Every dollar he saves is accumulating for some future need. If he accumulates enough dollars, he can miss a paycheck and not suffer. If he saves even more, he might miss an entire month and not suffer because the emergency fund is there to bridge the month's living expenses.

This logic is intuitive. What is less intuitive is the idea that all assets are really an inventory of time, with debt being its opposite. What you have accumulated in net worth will equate to some measure of time in relation to your chosen lifestyle. Lots of net worth equals lots of stored time, while a lavish lifestyle will consume that time faster than a modest one.

Whether our balance sheet is filled with cash, houses, or sophisticated investments, every asset is simply a different way of storing our real treasure called time. Through this lens, retirement planning becomes a simple program for storing time against later needs. And inheritance becomes a time capsule that passes wealth between generations. Time is one thing every person shares equally each day. Some choose to redeem it while others choose to waste it. A Prosperous Home aims to steward this treasure well.

EMERGENCY FUND

Emergency funds should be thought of like bumpers that absorb the impact of surprise calamities. Most Americans are undercapitalized, meaning millions of homes are crippled by debt and negative net worth. Capitalization means mounting net worth for a purpose. How much you mount is a matter of priorities. Many families spend more on playing than they do for saving. When unhappy times come, they depend upon borrowing to cover unplanned spending. This combination is able to destroy legacies and wealth.

The emergency fund makes a home stronger. As the emergency fund grows, the more robust a home grows, to the point of becoming its own bank without the need to borrow. When a home uses an emergency fund to resolve a crisis, then later manages to replenish the emergency fund to its pre-crisis balance, the cycle of debt is rendered powerless for that home.

The size of your emergency fund should match the threats you are trying to defend against. For example, as a college student, my emergency fund was around $200. This was enough to replace a stolen or destroyed college textbook or pay a minor medical bill at a campus health clinic. When I married, our emergency fund grew to around $1,000 for joint emergencies. As children came along, our emergency fund grew again to around $2,500. As my sons became teens, my emergency fund grew again to around $5,000.

Most emergency funds are confused with special needs money, but the two are very different. Emergencies are calamities like accidents and injuries; they are sudden and important. Special needs feel urgent, but are not emergencies. The forgotten birthday gift or last-minute shopping impulse are foreseeable and manageable. Bald tires and dead car batteries are maintenance needs, not emergencies. You should plan for needs within your LGS and use the emergency fund to solve actual calamities. If needed, invite a trusted friend or mentor to guide your thinking on the important difference between an emergency and a special need.

LIFE-BRIDGE BALANCE SHEET

If we accept the idea that assets are a way to inventory time, then we can further accept that inventoried time is a way to pass wealth across generations. Understanding wealth as stored time can sharpen what we keep or sell, and how we accumulate for generations that follow.

The rich man is always after more; the prosperous soul is always after purpose. Balance sheets are one quantitative tool for measuring time in terms of money. To demonstrate a qualitative model, we must speak in terms identity and purpose, and once again circle back to our important work on the Purpose Train.

> *Therefore be careful how you walk, not as unwise men but as wise, making the most of your time, because the days are evil.*
>
> *Ephesians 5:15-16 NASB*

Refresh your Purpose Train and consider how those qualitative ideals would reshape your quantitative balance sheet. Could your balance sheet represent purpose across 200 or more years of stored time? Building a Life-Bridge Balance Sheet is a godly idea and a powerful challenge to a Prosperous Home. Bringing that 200-year idea into today will improve your strategic thinking and refine your tactics for long-term stewardship.

Maybe you have never thought of a Life-Bridge Balance Sheet before; maybe you have and it fuels fear. Either way, my point is this: understanding your purpose and making intentional choices to achieve it can be called supernatural stewardship. A home that operates this way can be called a Prosperous Home. The Jews aimed for vitality and so should we. Because without it, you aim at nothing. And we both know where that will take us:

But if anyone does not provide for his own, and especially for those of his household, he has denied the faith and is worse than an unbeliever.

1 Timothy 5:8 NASB

I invite you to build a Life-Bridge Balance Sheet according to God's leading. Settle how to build in your heart, then apply your faith and strength to accomplish it. Whatever you do, let it be done in faith. I offer this prayer to that end:

Father, I am grateful for the gospel. And I am grateful that You want me to be powerful in my life for the sake of the weak. Thank You that You made me neither a victim nor a villain, but a hero with my money. Thank You for granting me the courage to look at my assets and my debts. I put my finances in Your hands—truly, they have always been there. Bless me how You will, forgive me where I need, and strengthen me when I fear. By Your grace, I will steward this Prosperous Home. I ask this in Jesus' name. Amen.

LESSONS
CHAPTER ELEVEN

HOMEWORK

Pick an amount of time (10 years, 50 years, 200 years, 500 years) and build a Life-Bridge Balance Sheet to reflect that using the form found on the next page. Discuss your changing mindset with a friend.

VIDEO

Watch video #11 entitled, "Outsmarting the Balance Sheet," on your DVD or online curriculum.

Watch tutorial video #13 entitled, "Planning Family Income," on your DVD or online curriculum.

GOING DEEPER

How does switching from the income statement to the balance sheet give you a better perspective of your financial health?

How does thinking of money as time change your view of money?

What ways has God inspired you to create a Life-Bridge Balance Sheet of 10, 50, 200, or 500 years?

What practical steps could you take to create or build assets that outrun inflation?

How can you move from crisis-based finances to being in control of your finances and successfully riding the waves of life?

How does changing the idea of an emergency fund to only being used for unseen emergencies help you plan for life better?

How would setting up a Life-Bridge Balance Sheet affect the way you fund your children and grandchildren?

How would your life be different had your parents or grandparents set up a Life-Bridge Balance Sheet?

FURTHER STUDY

Read or memorize the following verses: Hebrews 5:12-14, Hebrews 11:6, 1 Timothy 5:8, Ephesians 5:15-16.

Read the book, The Storehouse Principle, by Al Jandl and Van Crouch, (CrossStaff Publishers, Broken Arrow, OK, 2004).

Use a search engine to find Christian articles on these key words: yield, inflation, bls.gov, legacy, inheritance, and emergency fund.

Schedule an appointment with a financial adviser. Discuss the 200-year investments and see if you are compatible. Shop financial advisers until you find one who supports your investment values.

PRAYER

Father God, thank You for the chance to create and leave legacies and establish new trends in my family. Help me to move from a crisis-based faith to a deep, ongoing relationship with You. Help me to treasure time and use it wisely.

PROPHETIC ACT

Give $10 to a family member in need as an act of establishing prosperity in your family.

LIFE-BRIDGE

BALANCE SHEET

	10 YEARS	50 YEARS	200 YEARS	500 YEARS
Cash on Hand				
Emergency Cash				
Savings for a New Car				
Car #1				
Car #2				
Jewelry				
Furniture & Antiques				
Home				
IRA Retirement Savings				
401k Retirement Savings				
TOTAL ASSETS				
Credit Card #1				
Credit Card #2				
Credit Card #3				
Car Loan #1				
Car Loan #2				
Home Mortgage				
TOTAL DEBTS				
NET WORTH				

NOTES

CHAPTER 12

LGS

LEGACY PLAN

We can test your Life-Bridge Balance Sheet in the same way we tested your Target Balance Sheet. This is done by projecting the annual LGS across future years to see how your plan plays out over time. Does your long-term LGS support your Life-Bridge Balance Sheet goal? This is an advanced exercise for reconciling what you are doing with what you should be doing.

A good man leaves an inheritance to his children's children, And the wealth of the sinner is stored up for the righteous.

Proverbs 13:22 NASB

Using the good work you've already done, list your current LGS as percentages and dollars. Until now you've worked with a monthly LGS; now, shift to an annual LGS by multiplying monthly results by 12. Here is an example of an annual LGS for someone at age 30. Write your own annual amounts alongside these as both percentages and dollars.

L	80%	$40,000
G	10%	$5,000
S	10%	$5,000
	100%	$50,000

Next, build a span through time using your annual LGS and a simple spreadsheet. The left-side labels are Living, Giving, and Saving, and progressive ages follow across the top. I recommend you plan enough columns from now until age 100. Here is a partial example.

	AGE: 30	AGE: 31	AGE: 32	AGE: 33	AGE: 34	AGE: 35	AGE: 36	AGE: 37
LIVING	40,000	40,000	40,000	40,000	40,000	40,000	40,000	40,000
GIVING	5,000	5,000	5,000	5,000	5,000	5,000	5,000	5,000
SAVING	5,000	5,000	5,000	5,000	5,000	5,000	5,000	5,000
TOTAL	50,000	50,000	50,000	50,000	50,000	50,000	50,000	50,000

This example covers eight years, and every year is exactly like the one before. If this were accurate, they could expect to watch net worth grow by $40,000 (annual Savings of $5,000 x 8 years = $40,000) by the time they are 37 years of age. However, this static pattern isn't a reasonable expectation because we live in a dynamic world subject to needs, wants, and environmental trials.

Needs	Plans for Living, Giving, Saving, and debt payoffs, etc.
Wants	Improvements, replacements, education, vacation, etc.
Trials	Inflation, recession, emergencies, etc.

Thinking ahead, what are some likely needs, wants, and trials you can anticipate in the coming years? If your family is growing, what new spending might that invite? Perhaps your car needs to be replaced, or your parents need medical care. Each of these ideas can be estimated and layered against your long-term savings.

Being an optimist, I also expect income to improve. And given enough time, your LGS Savings should eliminate your home mortgage which materially lowers your Living costs. Be sure to estimate all likely events as you develop your LGS span across time.

Using our earlier example, this person expects income to grow by 2% each year. He also hopes to buy a car using cash from savings stashed every year. How much will this person have for the new car at the end of age 37? Assume he remains at an LGS of 80/10/10, and the raises are evenly spread over his LGS. If he postpones the purchase of the car until age 38, his net worth could increase by $42,914.[19]

	AGE: 30	AGE: 31	AGE: 32	AGE: 33	AGE: 34	AGE: 35	AGE: 36	AGE: 37
LIVING (80%)	40,000	40,800	41,616	42,448	43,298	44,164	45,046	45,948
GIVING (10%)	5,000	5,100	5,202	5,306	5,412	5,520	5,631	5,743
SAVING (10%)	5,000	5,100	5,202	5,306	5,412	5,520	5,631	5,743
TOTAL	50,000	51,000	52,020	53,060	54,122	55,204	56,308	57,434

Another approach could be to aim all raises fully into savings. The compounding effect of 2% over each year's salary would translate to an increasing net worth of $69,148.[20] This is a considerably more aggressive LGS than 80/10/10. Every LGS approach has different costs and benefits. For this second approach, living and giving would remain fixed over 8 years, forcing a significant change in LGS percentages. Can you calculate what the ending LGS would become if he chose the latter approach?[21] Such information demonstrates the power of the Legacy LGS spreadsheet.

Decisions we make today can have profound effects as they play out over a lifetime. Money can multiply, but it can only be invested in one place at a time. The man's first approach spread the growing income across his whole LGS on an 80/10/10 basis, which slowed the rate of savings. The second approach accelerated savings but restricted him in terms of living and giving. This give-and-take tension should happen on purpose and not by accident. The technical term for this tension is called opportunity cost.

Investopedia.com[22] defines opportunity cost as the cost of an alternative that must be forgone in order to pursue a certain action. Said another way, opportunity cost is the measure of what you sacrifice when your money goes elsewhere. In our example, the second

19 *Sum of LGS saving: $5,000+5,100+5,202+5,306+5,412+5,520+5,631+5,743=$42,914.*

20 *Sum of LGS saving: $5,000+6,000+7,020+8,060+9,122+10,204+11,308+12,434=$69,148.*

21 *Age 37 LGS: 69/9/22 ($40,000/$57,434; $5,000/$57,434; $12,434/$57,434).*

22 *http://www.investopedia.com/terms/o/opportunitycost.asp#ixzz43xC1TPqL*

approach of saving every dollar as income grew, had an opportunity cost in terms of living dollars (69% rather than 80%) and in terms of giving dollars (9% rather that 10%) because he concentrated on saving dollars (22% rather than 10%).

Create your own LGS Legacy Spreadsheet beginning with this year's LGS. Across the top, label each column with your age from now till age 100. Think about normal lifetime milestones that you will likely come upon as you move from now forward through time.

Assign dollars to those events using your own best guesses. Here are some typical life events to stimulate your thinking. Use these or create your own to sketch a reasonably accurate LGS Legacy Spreadsheet.

Plans for marriage
Birth of children
Private school tuition
College tuition
Buy a home with mortgage
Buy an auto using debt
Pay off auto loan
Pay off home mortgage
Change in career
Changes to LGS percentages
Start a business
Receive an inheritance
Philanthropy plans
Home improvement plans
Retirement
Social security benefits
Parental care needs
Move to new city or country

As you move through your LGS Legacy Spreadsheet, remember to keep inflows equal to outflows. If you do foresee seasons of borrowing (like seasons for college or starting a business), make plans to lower net worth as little as possible. Using the idea of opportunity cost, watch how life events affect your Living, Giving, and Saving over long arcs of time. Keep the 10,000-foot perspective for this exercise so you don't bog down with details.

Once you complete your first draft LGS Legacy Spreadsheet, think of it as an organic plan that can be adapted and refined as you move through time. One refinement that should be considered is inflation. Because you are looking across so many years, living costs will need to grow just to maintain a relative lifestyle. For example, living on $40,000 was extravagant in 1960, common in 2010, and will likely be less than half the poverty threshold by 2060.[23]

23 *US Census Bureau Table 1: Weighted Average Poverty Thresholds for Families of Specified Size: 1959 to 2014 shows the poverty threshold for a family of four in 1960 at $3,022 and in 2010 at $22,315. In 50 years, it will require nearly $100,000 to purchase the same living as 2010. My calculation is crude but illustrative, using a flat inflation projection of only 3%.*

You see how informed ideas can be expressed in LGS dollars for each year into the future. I used this exercise to see how efficiently I was in building my children's inheritance. Before I did this the first time, I had imagined leaving an inheritance of $1 million. One day it occurred that I had never applied my investment strategies and life plans to my LGS Legacy Spreadsheet to see if the dream had a sound underlying logic. At the time, my cash was invested at a safe but low rate of return. Debt was gone except for my home mortgage. Cash was accumulating and I needed to learn how to choose smarter investments.

My LGS was 80/10/10 in those days, which created an increase to net worth of around $5,000 each year. My strategy was to carry this annual amount across the coming years until reaching age 100, and see if my million-dollar expectation was sound. The end result was...not even close.

I laughed aloud when I recognized my overly conservative investment strategy and how my 80/10/10 LGS did not support my millionaire rhetoric. It felt like God was smiling at my child-like naiveté. He was willing to help, but as a steward I would need to grow.

In the end, think about where you are and whether your LGS strategy is driving net worth up or down. Study this across the arc of your lifetime and prayerfully adapt your strategies as a supernatural steward. We know the actual results depend completely on God, but our part can be faith-filled and proactive. Remember, good stewardship happens on purpose, not by accident.

> *Instruct those who are rich in this present world not to be conceited or to fix their hope on the uncertainty of riches, but on God, who richly supplies us with all things to enjoy. Instruct them to do good, to be rich in good works, to be generous and ready to share, storing up for themselves the treasure of a good foundation for the future, so that they may take hold of that which is life indeed.*
>
> *1 Timothy 6:17-19 NASB*

LESSONS

CHAPTER TWELVE

HOMEWORK

Fill out the LGS Legacy Spreadsheet found on the next page.

VIDEO

Watch video #12 entitled, "LGS Legacy Plan," on your DVD or online curriculum.

GOING DEEPER

How does planning out your LGS Legacy Spreadsheet help you steward your wealth better?

How does planning out future expenses help you better prepare for different expenses you might experience in different ages of your life?

What different ways could you build out an LGS to fulfill your purpose?

How does understanding opportunity cost change the way you view decisions you have made or are going to make in your life?

What inheritance are you hoping to leave to your family? How does your LGS Legacy Spreadsheet help or hinder that?

What ways to you feel God inviting you to stretch or grow in regarding your finances?

FURTHER STUDY

Read or memorize the following verses: Proverbs 13:22, 1 Timothy 6:17-19.

Use a search engine to find articles on these key words: ROI, return on investment, legacy.

Project a long-term result of your investments, including your home. Use that information to make a better plan and revisit it each year as a family gathering.

PRAYER

Lord Jesus, thank You that You have good plans for me, plans for me to prosper, to have hope and a future. Give me wisdom and divine strategy to create wealth in my life and leave an inheritance for my kids' kids.

PROPHETIC ACT

Memorize this verse every day this week, "THANK YOU GOD THAT YOU HAVE GOOD PLANS FOR ME, PLANS FOR ME TO PROSPER AND PLANS FOR ME TO HAVE HOPE AND A FUTURE" (Jeremiah 29:11).

LGS

LEGACY SPREADSHEET

	AGE:	AGE:	AGE:	AGE:	AGE:	AGE:	AGE:
LIVING							
GIVING							
SAVING							
TOTAL							

	AGE:	AGE:	AGE:	AGE:	AGE:	AGE:	AGE:
LIVING							
GIVING							
SAVING							
TOTAL							

	AGE:	AGE:	AGE:	AGE:	AGE:	AGE:	AGE:
LIVING							
GIVING							
SAVING							
TOTAL							

	AGE:	AGE:	AGE:	AGE:	AGE:	AGE:	AGE:
LIVING							
GIVING							
SAVING							
TOTAL							

	AGE:	AGE:	AGE:	AGE:	AGE:	AGE:	AGE:
LIVING							
GIVING							
SAVING							
TOTAL							

	AGE:	AGE:	AGE:	AGE:	AGE:	AGE:	AGE:
LIVING							
GIVING							
SAVING							
TOTAL							

	AGE:	AGE:	AGE:	AGE:	AGE:	AGE:	AGE:
LIVING							
GIVING							
SAVING							
TOTAL							

	AGE:	AGE:	AGE:	AGE:	AGE:	AGE:	AGE:
LIVING							
GIVING							
SAVING							
TOTAL							

	AGE:	AGE:	AGE:	AGE:	AGE:	AGE:	AGE:
LIVING							
GIVING							
SAVING							
TOTAL							

NOTES

CHAPTER 13

BIBLICAL
BORROWING AND LENDING

Few topics can match the emotional intensity and intellectual rigor required in understanding borrowing and lending. Opinions of debt are so disparate that many accept it as inevitable, unsure of its vice or virtue. Many Americans rely on borrowed money every day to make ends meet and while some use it carefully, others find themselves mired to the point of despair. One uses borrowing like a safety net while another looks more like an addict with his drug of choice.

Rules and tips will not resolve the problem of debt. The solution rests upon the idea of liberty, which I define as the capacity to choose. A failure in liberty will always return that person to bondage. Borrowing is another spiritual power, and hidden lies and wounds will always exaggerate it once debt becomes available. If needed, seek a Financial Sozo on the issue or find professional help in healing any lies that fuel debt addiction or dependence. Every believer has much to hope for and liberty is one of those promises. Let's turn now to understanding what the Bible says about borrowing and lending.

THE BIBLE ON DEBT

When I set to this task, I realized that nearly every idea I held regarding lending and borrowing came from the opinions of other teachers and not from my own research. True, these teachers were respectable and their opinions likely to be reliable, but I needed my own sound wisdom from my favorite source: the Bible.

The Bible has many references to borrowing and lending, but often those contextually relate to other topics. For example, Moses forbade charging interest to the poor, but this law had more to do with charity and the Hebrew welfare system than being a guideline for institutional borrowing and lending.

> *If you lend money to My people, to the poor among you, you are not to act as a creditor to him; you shall not charge him interest. If you ever take your neighbor's cloak as a pledge, you are to return it to him before the sun sets, for that is his only covering; it is his cloak for his body. What else shall he sleep in? And it shall come about that when he cries out to Me, I will hear him, for I am gracious.*
>
> *Exodus 22:25-27*

The Bible is not a book on moneylending, but rather about living and knowing our Father in heaven. It is about a nation set apart, learning how to function under a heavenly system very different than systems common to humanity. Israel's economics depended upon financial vigor for all her people. Any person or families unable to support themselves to a certain standard were considered poor and eligible to receive charity directly from other Jews.

Where an American believer may limit the scope of charity to churches and non-profit organizations, the Jew understood giving to be much wider. Giving to family members and strangers, even loaning money to the poor, all had high merit with God. The point behind every gift or loan was to end dependence and enable self-sufficiency in the receiver. It is for these reasons that I see the verse above as aligning closer to a benevolence law than a moneylending law.

For my biblical studies, I chose the following key words[24] in an effort to understand God's best regarding borrowing and lending. Here are the words and a grouping of results to assist your own conclusions.

Borrow	Debt	Lending
Borrows	Debts	Lent
Borrowed	Indebted	Moneylending
Borrowing	Lend	Usury
Borrower	Lends	Usurer

GROUP 1 OF 7: DEMANDS OR GRANTS

The following verses refer to something closer akin to a demand or grant than institutional lending or borrowing. In context, these verses relate to plundering or surrendering where repayment isn't really part of the equation.

> *But every woman shall borrow of her neighbor, and of her that sojourneth in her house, jewels of silver, and jewels of gold, and raiment: and ye shall put them upon your sons, and upon your daughters; and ye shall spoil [PLUNDER] the Egyptians.*
>
> *Exodus 3:22 CWS*

> *Speak now in the ears of the people, and let every man borrow of his neighbor, and every woman of her neighbor, jewels of silver, and jewels of gold.*
>
> *Exodus 11:2 CWS*

> *And the children of Israel did according to the word of Moses; and they borrowed of the Egyptians jewels of silver, and jewels of gold, and raiment:*
>
> *Exodus 12:35 CWS*

24 *I chose NASB for ease of reading and CWS for its exceptional Hebrew and Greek word studies.*

And the Lord gave the people favor in the sight of the Egyptians, so that they lent unto them such things as they required. And they spoiled the Egyptians.

Exodus 12:36 CWS

But thou shalt open thine hand wide unto him, and shalt surely lend him sufficient for his need, in that which he wanteth.

Deuteronomy 15:8 CWS

Then he said, Go, borrow thee vessels abroad of all thy neighbors, even empty vessels; borrow not a few.

2 Kings 4:3 CWS

Give to him that asketh thee, and from him that would borrow of thee turn not thou away.

Matthew 5:42 CWS

And he said unto them, Which of you shall have a friend, and shall go unto him at midnight, and say unto him, Friend, lend me three loaves;

Luke 11:5 CWS

2 OF 7: CONDITION OF EXPLOITATION

These verses are closer akin to a condition of exploitation than institutional lending or borrowing. In context, these verses relate to judgment, suffering or discontent. Because the word debt is used, we can deduce that debtors serve their lenders.

Be not thou one of them that strike hands, or of them that are sureties for debts.

Proverbs 22:26 CWS

And every one that was in distress, and every one that was in debt, and every one that was discontented, gathered themselves unto him; and he became a captain over them: and there were with him about four hundred men.

1 Samuel 22:2 CWS

And it shall be, as with the people, so with the priest; as with the servant, so with his master; as with the maid, so with her mistress; as with the buyer, so with the seller; as with the lender, so with the borrower; as with the taker of usury, so with the giver of usury to him.

Isaiah 24:2 CWS

Woe is me, my mother, that thou hast borne me a man of strife and a man of contention to the whole earth! I have neither lent on usury, yet every one of them doth curse me.

Jeremiah 15:10 CWS

3 OF 7: REMUNERATION AND RESTITUTION

These verses are closer akin to contract law regarding remuneration and restitution than to institutional lending or borrowing. Indirectly we can learn to communicate with honor toward the person at disadvantage. People are more important than things.

And if a man borrow aught of his neighbor, and it be hurt, or die, the owner thereof being not with it, he shall surely make it good.

Exodus 22:14 CWS

When thou dost lend thy brother any thing, thou shalt not go into his house to fetch his pledge.

Deuteronomy 24:10 CWS

Thou shalt stand abroad, and the man to whom thou dost lend shall bring out the pledge abroad unto thee.

Deuteronomy 24:11 CWS

But as one was felling a beam, the axe head fell into the water: and he cried, and said, Alas, master! for it was borrowed.

2 Kings 6:5 CWS

Now to him that worketh is the reward not reckoned of grace, but of debt.

Romans 4:4 CWS

4 OF 7: DEDICATION TO GOD

These verses are closer akin to the dedication of a person to the Lord than institutional lending or borrowing. When someone is dedicated to serving God at birth, the Bible calls this being lent to the Lord.

Therefore also I have lent him to the Lord; as long as he liveth he shall be lent to the Lord. And he worshiped the Lord there.

1 Samuel 1:28 CWS

And Eli blessed Elkanah and his wife, and said, The Lord give thee seed of this woman for the loan which is lent to the Lord. And they went unto their own home.

1 Samuel 2:20 CWS

5 OF 7: MORAL FAULTS

These verses are closer akin to moral faults than institutional lending or borrowing. These verses are related to sin and salvation. Our pre-Christian condition is a debt of separation our works could never repay.

> *And forgive us our debts, as we forgive our debtors.*
>
> *Matthew 6:12 CWS*

> *And forgive us our sins; for we also forgive every one that is indebted to us. And lead us not into temptation; but deliver us from evil.*
>
> *Luke 11:4 CWS*

6 OF 7: KINGDOM ECONOMY

These verses are closer akin to illustrating how a kingdom economy operates than institutional lending or borrowing. These verses are related to faithfulness, mercy, and Sabbath rather than literal laws about money. This is similar to the fig tree parable and the "seventy times seven" lesson of Jesus. These verses are instructional but break down as instructional debt principles. I do believe God wishes for us to all be debt-free, just as He wishes us all to live without sin. But in the interim of life, liberty permits us to take on and repay debt without guilt or condemnation.

> *For the Lord thy God blesseth thee, as he promised thee: and thou shalt lend unto many nations, but thou shalt not borrow; and thou shalt reign over many nations, but they shall not reign over thee.*
>
> *Deuteronomy 15:6 CWS*

The Lord shall open unto thee his good treasure, the heaven to give the rain unto thy land in his season, and to bless all the work of thine hand: and thou shalt lend unto many nations, and thou shalt not borrow.

Deuteronomy 28:12 CWS

He shall lend to thee, and thou shalt not lend to him: he shall be the head, and thou shalt be the tail.

Deuteronomy 28:44 CWS

Then she came and told the man of God. And he said, Go, sell the oil, and pay thy debt, and live thou and thy children of the rest.

2 Kings 4:7 CWS

The rich ruleth over the poor, and the borrower is servant to the lender.

Proverbs 22:7 CWS

And if the people of the land bring ware or any victuals on the Sabbath day to sell, that we would not buy it of them on the Sabbath, or on the holy day: and that we would leave the seventh year, and the exaction of every debt.

Nehemiah 10:31 CWS

Thou oughtest therefore to have put my money to the exchangers, and then at my coming I should have received mine own with usury.

Matthew 25:27 CWS

Then the lord of that servant was moved with compassion and loosed him, and forgave him the debt.

Matthew 18:27 CWS

And he would not: but went and cast him into prison, till he should pay the debt.

Matthew 18:30 CWS

Then his lord, after that he had called him, said unto him, O thou wicked servant, I forgave thee all that debt, because thou desiredst me: Shouldest not thou also have had compassion on thy fellow servant, even as I had pity on thee? And his lord was wroth, and delivered him to the tormentors, till he should pay all that was due unto him. So likewise shall my heavenly Father do also unto you, if ye from your hearts forgive not every one his brother their trespasses.

Matthew 18:32-35 CWS

And if ye lend to them of whom ye hope to receive, what thank have ye? for sinners also lend to sinners, to receive as much again. But love ye your enemies, and do good, and lend, hoping for nothing again; and your reward shall be great, and ye shall be the children of the Highest: for he is kind unto the unthankful and to the evil.

Luke 6:34-35 CWS

Wherefore then gavest not thou my money into the bank, that at my coming I might have required mine own with usury?

Luke 19:23 CWS

7 OF 7: INTEREST AND USURY

Usury in America means exorbitant interest rates, whereas Scripture indicates that all interest is usurious. Old Testament law prohibited all interest between Jews for the use of money, food, tools, and even capital across time, but permitted interest on loans to foreigners. The prohibition of interest among Jews was a powerful economic engine to a tiny tribal nation living among larger and often hostile neighbors. Even today, low interest rates are considered a useful tool for stimulating a nation's economy. The availability of low- or zero-interest lending entices many entrepreneurs to risk startups and expansions. Imagine the incentive in an economic system stimulated by zero-rate loans among its nation's risk-takers.

> *He that hath not given forth upon usury, neither hath taken any increase, that hath withdrawn his hand from iniquity, hath executed true judgment between man and man,*
>
> *Ezekiel 18:8 CWS*

> *Hath given forth upon usury, and hath taken increase: shall he then live? he shall not live: he hath done all these abominations; he shall surely die; his blood shall be upon him.*
>
> *Ezekiel 18:13 CWS*

> *That hath taken off his hand from the poor, that hath not received usury nor increase, hath executed my judgments, hath walked in my statutes; he shall not die for the iniquity of his father, he shall surely live.*
>
> *Ezekiel 18:17 CWS*

> *In thee have they taken gifts to shed blood; thou hast taken usury and increase, and thou hast greedily gained of thy neighbors by extortion, and hast forgotten me, saith the Lord God.*
>
> *Ezekiel 22:12 CWS*

> *If thou lend money to any of my people that is poor by thee, thou shalt not be to him as a usurer, neither shalt thou lay upon him usury.*
>
> *Exodus 22:25 CWS*

> *Take thou no usury of him, or increase: but fear thy God; that thy brother may live with thee.*
>
> *Leviticus 25:36 CWS*

Thou shalt not give him thy money upon usury, nor lend him thy victuals for increase.

Leviticus 25:37 CWS

Thou shalt not lend upon usury of money, usury of victuals, usury of any thing that is lent upon usury:

Deuteronomy 23:19 CWS

Unto a stranger thou mayest lend upon usury; but unto thy brother thou shalt not lend upon usury: that the Lord thy God may bless thee in all that thou settest thine hand to in the land whither thou goest to possess it.

Deuteronomy 23:20 CWS

There were also that said, We have borrowed money for the king's tribute, and that upon our lands and vineyards.

Nehemiah 5:4 CWS

Then I consulted with myself, and I rebuked the nobles, and the rulers, and said unto them, Ye exact usury, every one of his brother. And I set a great assembly against them.

Nehemiah 5:7 CWS

I likewise, and my brethren, and my servants, might exact of them money and corn: I pray you, let us leave off this usury.

Nehemiah 5:10 CWS

He that putteth not out his money to usury, nor taketh reward against the innocent. He that doeth these things shall never be moved.

Psalms 15:5 CWS

He that by usury and unjust gain increaseth his substance, he shall gather it for him that will pity the poor.

Proverbs 28:8 CWS

HOW MUCH BONDAGE?

In conclusion, these verses grant permission for believers to lend and borrow, but bring the usage of debt to a much finer point than most of us understand. Debt should not be used for daily living or consumption. We are not to enslave ourselves to lenders by carrying ponderous amounts of borrowing. We are not to charge interest among ourselves. And we are to work to bring the poor out of poverty by helping them become self-sufficient.

Pointedly, I believe a biblical use of debt should be reserved for starting business ventures,gaining education, acquiring major assets like homes and investments, and funding major life events such as weddings, college, and illness. Whether interest can be charged always depends upon the identity of the borrower, and rates may range from zero to fair market. Finally, understand that the Jewish system loaned within families and friends and seldom involved third-party institutions. Israel had a seven-year cycle of sabbatical years and a 70-year cycle for jubilee that systematically released certain debts and returned certain assets to their genealogical owners. America has no equivalent short of bankruptcy, foreclosure, and repossession laws. Whether biblical or secular, borrowing is always a form of bondage and is never without risk. I believe borrowing is not the best route, but it can be considered an option for believers who are seeking strictly biblical guidance.

Many years ago, I was asking God for wisdom for a leveraged investment strategy. After all my words were spent, I sat quietly listening. I heard the Holy Spirit ask me this question: A little debt means a little bondage. A lot of debt means a lot of bondage. How much bondage are you willing to live with?

It was a direct question, and its answer has guided my decisions ever since. I will explain how I worked through that idea in the next chapter but understand that all this biblical study on debt only brings us around to the matter of liberty. It is a choice to use or not use debt. The real question will be what the power of borrowing is going to exaggerate within you.

> *And He said to them, "Because of the littleness of your faith; for truly I say to you, if you have faith the size of a mustard seed, you will say to this mountain, 'Move from here to there,' and it will move; and nothing will be impossible to you."*
>
> *Matthew 17:20 NASB*

LESSONS
CHAPTER THIRTEEN

HOMEWORK

Study Stephen's Wealth Map at the end of this chapter. Consider how these different layers reflect a descending importance from the top down. Where are your efforts focused?

VIDEO

Watch video #13 entitled, "Biblical Borrowing and Lending," on your DVD or online curriculum.

GOING DEEPER

What was your view on debt?

What scripture or group of scripture surprised you most?

In your opinion, what is a good use of debt and what is a bad use of debt?

What does a kingdom economy look like?

Create your own philosophy on debt and borrowing. Write it out on the next page.

How does Jewish economics differ from your country's economics and what practices would you adopt from Jewish economics?

How does the Bible's view of poverty and taking care of family change your view of charity?

FURTHER STUDY

Read or memorize a verse of your choice from Chapter 13 above.

Use a search engine to find Christian articles on these key words: debt, borrowing, and leveraging.

Summarize your position on debt in one or two sentences. Add supporting scripture and share your conclusions with a friend.

PRAYER

Father God, thank You for being my provider. Thank You for raising my knowledge on what debt is and Your desires for a kingdom economy. Give me wisdom on how to understand debt, get out of debt, and live a life free from bondage. Show me what my philosophy on debt should be.

PROPHETIC ACT

Spend five minutes or more dancing with or without music as an act of stating your life is a life of freedom. For a more difficult challenge, dance in front of people you don't know.

WEALTH MAP

ADOPTION [IDENTITY]

Rom. 8:15 …you have received a spirit of adoption as sons…

God made us significant when we accepted His salvation.

HERITAGE [YOUR TREASURY]

Luke 12:34 For where your treasure is, there your heart will be also.

Peace	Home Order	Sound Sleep
Good Name	Honor	Friendships
Integrity	Confidence	

WISDOM [YOUR GARDEN]

Philippians 4:8 Finally, brethren, whatever is true, honorable, right, pure, lovely…

Health	Prophetic Words	Diligence
Experience	Dreams/Passions	Perseverance
Education	Social Skills	Focus & Intention
Training	Scripture Library	Sabbath
Talents/Abilities	Security	Legacy
Alliances	Traditions	Generosity

SERVICE [YOUR PLATFORM]

Mark 16:15 And He said to them, "Go…."

City/Region (Citizenship)
Home (Family Leadership)
Work (Marketplace Leadership)
Church (Body of Christ)
Missions (World Leadership)
Government (Political Leadership)
Boardsmanship (Organizational Leadership)

MONEY [YOUR ASSETS]

Matthew 6:33 …and all these things will be added to you.

DooDads
Cash/Equivalents
Certificates Deposit
Treasuries
Stocks/Bonds
Land
Improvements
Home Equity
Life Insurance CSV
Annuities
Commercial Paper/Trust Deeds
Mineral Rights
Intellectual Property
Collectibles
Metals/Gems
Commodities
Ventures And Capital
Currencies

NOTES

CHAPTER 14

WORKING FREE FROM DEBT

We live in a culture fixated on spending and consumption. Governments, economists, and marketers all support a relentless drumming of consumerism as a path to unlimited prosperity and happiness. This message is false, yet it persists for one very simple reason: Americans want their stuff. There is no other nation even close to our level of per-capita consumption—and that is not a boast. No one is forcing our families into debt; we enslave ourselves willingly and persistently.

As believers, we are meant to be debt-free. Biblically, debt and borrowing are not sins; however borrowing is a form of bondage. A little debt means a little bondage, and lots of debt means lots of bondage. How much bondage are you willing to live with? My answer to God's question was zero bondage, so I set to the difficult task of paying off debt. The process took me much longer than expected, but Dawna and I did eventually repay all our loans.

The early years of our marriage generated credit card balances, car loans, and home mortgages with ease. These were the years of "easy credit" and nearly every advisor and consumer ran after debt like it was the newest and greatest tactic for creating sudden wealth. Historically this nation-wide approach to borrowing contributed to a quickening bulge to the middle class balance sheet. Unfortunately the assets gained were matched with debts. We called it "leverage," which is much nicer sounding than borrowing or bondage. Government policies were loosened, institutional procedures were adapted, and consumers grew insatiable in their appetite for more. But assets are not the same as wealth, and although Dawna and I were caught up in the rush to riches, we slowed long enough to listen to the Father in heaven. His answer came softly: How much bondage are you willing to live with?

> *So also we, while we were children, were held in bondage under the elemental things of the world.*
>
> *Galatians 4:3 NASB*

When Dawna and I set to the task of reducing debt, we found ourselves caught between two polarizing ideals. On one side, voices encouraged borrowing for investment and tax reasons. The other side categorically condemned any borrowing, which left us feeling condemned ourselves. In the end, we listened to neither one, but accepting God's invitation to zero bondage.

Now, we think of debt as a tool that is temporary and helpful in passing through storms. But as a Tactic, debt is not a wise choice over long periods. I use debt in seasons, and work to escape as quickly as possible. Consequently, Dawna and I ended up repaying debt in stages, alternating between extra loan payments and cash accumulation. God consistently defended our emergency fund, while always focusing our eyes on protecting net worth. This experience will echo through the story that follows—protecting net worth and preserving stability became our slow march to financial freedom. Here is one story to illustrate our short-term use of credit.

My son once crashed his pickup in a pounding rain storm. It was frightful and, thanks to God, he was unhurt. But after the accident, the vehicle was ruined. He lived hundreds of miles from home finishing college so we needed to replace the vehicle as quickly as possible. The replacement of a vehicle exceeded our emergency fund, but not our borrowing capacity. We decided to pay a large down payment using our emergency fund and borrow the rest. For our son's part, he now owed us the money while we carried the institutional loan responsibility. Immediately before the accident, our balance sheet looked like this.

+Emergency Cash	$5,000
+Old Pickup Truck	$10,000
-Debt	-0
=Net Worth	$15,000

Immediately after the crash, our balance sheet looked like this. We still had the cash but the value of the original truck was lost

Emergency Cash	$5,000
+Old Pickup Truck	0
-Debt	-0
=Net Worth	$5,000

We made our down payment and borrowed the remainder, placing my son's new car on the balance sheet as follows.

Emergency Cash	$1,000
+New Pickup Truck	9,000
-Debt	-5,000
=Net Worth	$5,000

First, notice that we didn't use all of our emergency fund. This was because we never again wanted to risk entrapment in a debt cycle. Unexpected things can be anticipated, and for a short season we were willing to live at a minimum exposure of $1,000 emergency fund. We've never permitted ourselves an emergency fund of zero. This became our personal risk boundary.

Second, notice that his new truck did not damage our net worth, even though we borrowed. The original accident caused a loss of $10,000. Losing the truck damaged our net worth, but we were not willing to damage it further by borrowing beyond the original value. These are hypothetical numbers to demonstrate how our decision to replace the old truck was guided by something more than the cash flow equation. This is a triumph of balance sheet affluence over income statement affluence. Had we been income statement affluent, our decision would have centered on the interest rate and our capacity to pay a new auto loan payment. Of course we considered those details, but only as secondary matters.

In the months that followed, we aimed our LGS at rebuilding our emergency fund, while temporarily accepting the minimum monthly debt payments. This may seem counter-intuitive, but once our emergency fund recovered the $4,000 down payment, we then redirected our LGS to rapidly pay down the new truck debt. We were debt-free within seven months, turning a tragedy into a blessing and rebuilding our balance sheet. This is one testimony and experience from a Prosperous Home; it can become your testimony as well. My intention here is not to promote debt, but show how we personally used debt as a short-term tool. If you are persuaded to live on a cash-only basis, I celebrate your decision. May God bless whatever works for your Prosperous Home.

DEBT TERMINATOR

The debt terminator is a common and proven method for paying off debt. Begin by lifting your balances owed from your balance sheet and placing them in Columns 1 and 2. The debts should be listed from smallest to largest based on outstanding balance.

Next, enter the interest rates for each loan in Column 3, along with minimum monthly payments in Column 5. Column 4 is calculated by multiplying the balance by the monthly interest rate (it is likely Column 3 shows an annual rate, so divide it by 12 to get a simple monthly rate). For example, credit card 1 outstanding balance of $240 x its annual rate of 19% divided by 12 months equals the Column 4 interest charged this month on the balance ($240 x .19 / 12 mos. = $3.80).

Study the chart below. See if you can prove my figures in Columns 4 and 7.

Lender or Bank	Current Balance	Interest Rate(%)	Interest Charges	Minimum Payment	Extra Payment	Balance After
	+		+	-	-	=
Credit Card 1	$240	19%	$3.80	$3.00	$150.00	$90.80
Credit Card 2	$1,100	21%	$19.25	$18.00		$1,101.25
Credit Card 3	$2,400	8%	$16.00	$12.00		$2,404.00
Other Loan	$9,000	11%	$82.50	$80.00		$9,002.50
Home Mort.	$240,000	6%	$1,200.00	$1,438.92		$239,761.08

Resist the temptation to list loans in order of interest rates. The power of the debt terminator is in payoff momentum and listing the smallest loans first creates this most efficiently. Each month, the eliminated loans free up minimum payments as the momentum begins. As debts are paid off, the terminator gathers size and momentum toward the next largest loan. This continues until all debts are repaid. You can refine your approach later; for now, practice the basics by listing debts from smallest to largest and not worrying about the interest rates.

Remember the funnel? Column 6 is the extra amount applied toward debt, and this comes from the Savings part of the LGS. Any amount directed at debt can be placed into the Debt Terminator worksheet Column 6. Below is the same example as above, except the first loan is now paid off and the second loan is now under attack by the strength of its own minimum payment (Credit card 2 Column 5), plus the minimum payment now freed by the first loan payoff (Credit card 1 Column 5), plus the LGS amount being aimed at the debt (Column 6). See if you can estimate how many more payments will be needed to eliminate Credit card 2. On and on this goes each month, until the terminator method wipes out debt.

Lender or Bank	Current Balance	Interest Rate(%)	Interest Charges	Minimum Payment	Extra Payment	Balance After
	+		+	-	-	=
Credit Card 1	$90.80	19%	$1.44	$3.00	$89.28	0.00
Credit Card 2	$1,101.25	21%	$19.27	$21.00	$60.72	$1,038.80
Credit Card 3	$2,404.00	8%	$16.03	$12.00		$2,408.03
Other Loan	$9,002.50	11%	$82.52	$80.00		$9,005.02
Home Mort.	$239,761.08	6%	$1,198.81	$1,438.92		$239,520.97

BRAVE TO SEE

Part of discovering one's financial condition is looking at information that is sometimes troubling or disturbing. Gathering the sum total of one's debt might seem discouraging, but don't avoid this important step. The enemy would prefer us to hide from financial facts. Ignorance is not a gift of the Spirit. Self-condemnation is a favored tactic the devil uses against all victims. But we are not victims. We are heroes with knowledge, hope, and intention—three powerful weapons in a Prosperous Home.

> *Our soul has escaped as a bird out of the snare of the trapper; The snare is broken and we have escaped.*
>
> *Psalms 124:7 NASB*

LESSONS
CHAPTER FOURTEEN

HOMEWORK

Create your own Debt Terminator using the sheet found on the next page. If you have no debt, congratulations, you have no homework from this chapter!

VIDEO

Watch video #14 entitled, "Working Free From Debt," on your DVD or online curriculum.

GOING DEEPER

Does this idea of "how much bondage are you willing to live with" change the Priority List you created back in chapter 10?

Is the idea of never having a zero emergency fund something you would adopt? Why or why not?

How would the debt snowball help you in paying off debt?

Does looking at your debt scare you? If so, what can you do to overcome that fear?

How has this curriculum helped you in developing a Prosperous Home?

What has been the most difficult and the most inspiring part of this curriculum?

FURTHER STUDY

Read or memorize these verses: Psalms 124:7, Galatians 4:3.

Use a search engine and find articles on using a debt snowball.

Plan a celebration for when you pay off your first and last debts.

PRAYER

Lord Jesus, thank You that debt does not scare You. Thank You that You are working in my life to create a free and abundant life. Help me to create a strategy and follow it as I seek to have full financial freedom in my life.

PROPHETIC ACT

Take a piece of paper, crumple it up and wrap another piece of paper around it until you have the same amount of paper as you do different debts. Then, throw it away as an act of faith saying you are throwing away your debt. (If you are around snow, feel free to use snow.)

DEBT TERMINATOR

Lender or Bank	Current Balance	Interest Rate(%)	Interest Charges	Minimum Payment	Extra Payment	Balance After
	+		+	-	-	=

NOTES

CHAPTER 15

A CLOSING WORD

Congratulations for completing the Prosperous Home manual. Seek a small group or Prosperous Soul Coach to iron out any details or nuance as you apply this material to your unique circumstances. Set clear targets on your way to purpose and pray for God to bless the journey. Listen carefully and prayerfully to every advice that comes, but be true to what God is doing in your heart. Become ferocious in your supernatural stewardship, resilient to emotional storms and financial setbacks. Do this in faith and watch God's favor follow.

At the end of this chapter, you will find a Satisfaction Survey and Testimony Sheet. I would be honored to receive your feedback. Please consider completing the page and submitting it to my team for evaluation.

By now, you should be able to identify the key elements of net worth. You understand the LGS and can build a plan that supports your Target Balance Sheet. You can happen to life by using the Purpose Train and priority war tools. From here, you only require the ingredients of time and persistence to see financial success take root in your home. But this is only the beginning. From here, you can learn advanced skills of a Prosperous Home. You can grow in your ability to create wealth and steward it well according to God's will.

True Riches

Creating wealth summons images of multiplying streams of income and soaring net worth where value did not exist before. All this and more is possible with Christ. Yet in the face of all this potential, learn to protect your heart from presumption and greed. There are many biblical warnings about this error. Consider here the warning of scripture:

> *"Otherwise, you may say in your heart, 'My power and the strength of my hand made me this wealth.' But you shall remember the LORD your God, for it is He who is giving you power to make wealth, that He may confirm His covenant which He swore to your fathers, as it is this day."*
>
> *Deuteronomy 8:17-18 NASB*

Preserving our devotion to Christ becomes the greatest test in wealth. Skills can be learned, but the key to success hides within the caverns of the heart of man. We can steward with spiritual eyes. We can use the prophetic in our choices of investment. We can watch as our Father in heaven lengthens our stride within His will and good pleasure. But all this will continue to return us to the basic truth that our hearts are blenders without a lid.

Paul the apostle said it best. He was speaking to an adolescent church in the thriving center of Corinth. These believers were probably much like you and me, not former Jews but gentile men and women who found salvation in Jesus Christ. Their culture was not conducive to quiet Christian living. It was busy at their own race for riches. It is in this familiar bustle that Paul defends his apostleship:

> *But I am afraid that, as the serpent deceived Eve by his craftiness, your minds will be led astray from the simplicity and purity of devotion to Christ.*
>
> *2 Corinthians 11:3 NASB*

On a first reading, Paul appears not to speak of money. Yet between the lines, we can hear what Paul values most—a tender relationship with Jesus, which he describes as "the simplicity and purity of devotion to Christ."

This veteran servant of God, a teacher of teachers, reveals the formula for passing the test of wealth as keeping ourselves simple and pure and not thinking too highly of ourselves or our troubles. From such a posture, God can add power to our lives and demonstrate even more of Jesus in a troubled world.

These are the true riches Jesus described. This is the real stewardship, and one that the Holy Spirit can bless. Realize that our financial struggle, like all problems, will become impossible when we each arrive in heaven. Perhaps now is the only way to prove who we really are. As stewards, let's really be about souls and demonstrating the beauty of Christ's kingdom on earth. As in heaven, may God bless your Prosperous Home.

LESSONS
CHAPTER FIFTEEN

HOMEWORK

Help us build a world-class product. Complete the Satisfaction Survey and Testimony Sheet online, or email your results to *contactus@prosperoussoul.com.*

VIDEO

Watch video #15 entitled, "A Closing Word," on your DVD or online curriculum.

GOING DEEPER

How has this course affected your thinking about home finances?

What is one thing you will start doing as a result of this course?

What is one thing you will stop doing as a result of this course?

What is one thing you will change doing as a result of this course?

Is there someone you could share this manual with?

FURTHER STUDY

Read or memorize scripture every day.

Repeat this course one year from now.

Communicate your financial goals clearly to another person to whom you are accountable. Watch and return testimonies as God continues to bless your Prosperous Home.

PRAYER

Father in heaven, bless me that I might prosper and be in good health, even as my soul prospers (3 John 1:2). In Jesus' name I pray. Amen.

PROPHETIC ACT

Celebrate your achievement by planning a dinner out. It need not be lavish, only joyful and rewarding. God bless your prosperous soul.

NOTES

EXTRA WORKSHEETS

WORKSHEET LOCATOR

Chapter 1	CURIOUS LIST OF LIES
Chapter 2	PURPOSE TRAIN WORKSHEET
Chapter 3	BALANCE SHEET DISCOVERY
Chapter 4	TARGET BALANCE SHEET
Chapter 5	ACTIVE, PASSIVE, & VALUE INCOME WORKSHEET
Chapter 6	LIVING, GIVING, SAVING (LGS) WORKSHEET
Chapter 7	LGS PRACTISE SHEET
Chapter 8	LGS MASTER SHEET
Chapter 9	OFFERING READING #1
Chapter 10	PRIORITY WAR
Chapter 11	LIFE BRIDGE BALANCE SHEET
Chapter 12	LEGACY SPREADSHEET
Chapter 13	WEALTH MAP
Chapter 14	DEBT TERMINATOR

PROSPEROUSHOME

CHAPTER ONE

CURIOUS LIST OF LIES

I. LIES AGAINST OUR PROTECTION BY GOD (i.e. Fear of punishment)
...But Perfect Love Casts Out Fear (1 John 4:18).

- I live in constant fear about money;
  - God has not given me a spirit of fear (See 1 Timothy 1:7).

- Something has to go wrong because things are going too well;
  - God has a plan to prosper me and not harm me (See Jeremiah 29:11)

- My family is cursed. I am cursed and can't break free;
  - Family curses, after accepting Christ, were washed and cannot stick any longer (See proverbs 26:2).

- I am attacked and vulnerable. I am pressed on every side;
  - God is my strong tower where I can hide and be safe (See Proverbs 18:10).

- I'm afraid of money because it will rule me or ruin me;
  - God is able to protect and strengthen me from the evil one (2 Thessalonians 3:3).

- I feel condemned by mistakes and choices made. I'm guilty;
  - The Lord is faithful and able to forgive our sins, and wash us completely clean (See 1 John 1:9).

- Every time I win or gain, I fail or something happens to steal it and take it all away;
  -God will protect me and keep me from tests that are beyond me. He will provide an escape every time I need it (See 1 Corinthians 10:13).

CHAPTER ONE

(CONTINUED)

II. LIES AGAINST OUR PROVISION BY GOD (i.e. Fear of abandonment)
...But God will supply all that I need from His great treasury (See Philippians 4:19).

- My past mistakes have ruined my future; I have nothing left to give;
  - God will give me seed when I need seed, and bread when I need bread (See 2 Corinthians 9:10).

- It's too late for me; I'm too old to change;
  - God's promises apply to me regardless of age (See Genesis 17:17).

- I shouldn't ask for things, and when I do I'm ignored or put in my place;
  - I can ask God in confidence, knowing He wants to hear from me (See 1 John 5:14).

- God is too big and too busy to pay attention to me;
  - God's eye is upon me. I am not forgotten (See Luke 12:24).

- I am jobless and can't find work;
  - God will supply all my needs (See Philippians 4:19).

- I can't follow the Lord and have money too;
  - I am a servant of Christ and a steward of His mysteries (See 1 Corinthians 4:1).

- I ask for blessing but nothing ever comes. I'm overlooked by God's promises;
  - God is able to make all grace abound to me, so I always have what I need in every way (See 2 Corinthians 9:8).

CHAPTER ONE

(CONTINUED)

III. LIES AGAINST OUR IDENTITY AS HEIRS OF GOD (i.e. Damaged or missing self worth and identity) ...But the Holy Spirit testifies with our own spirit that I am a child of God (See Romans 8:16).

- I am insignificant, what can I do?
  - I can do all things in Christ because He makes my efforts strong (See Ephesians 1:10).

- I always feel rejected by people, by God, by my self;
  - The cross qualifies me to draw near to God with confidence (See Hebrews 4:16).

- I'm too stupid to understand money. What I think doesn't matter;
  - My ideas matter because I have the mind of Christ (See 1 Corinthians 2:16).

- I'm so deep in debt, God can never help me. God would never help me because I don't deserve to be helped.
  - God so loves me, that He sent His only son to pay for my errors (See John 3:16).

- I've always been behind others. I will never succeed because I'm just a worker;
  - I am no longer a slave, but a son/daughter. That makes me an heir of all the riches of heaven (See Galatians 4:7).

- I'm not dedicated enough. I can't hear God. It's safer not to try than to fail.
  - God is so great that He is building me up to be chosen for God's own possession (See 1 Peter 2:5-9).

- What can I do? I'm only flesh and blood and the world is such a big dark place;
  - I have been invited to stand beside God and create heaven on earth. This is what it means to be a friend and heir with Christ, full of wisdom and able to bear fruit in every good work (See Colossians 1:9-14).

CHAPTER TWO

PURPOSE TRAIN WORKSHEET

Pg. 34

PURPOSE

In the space below, come up with some words and ideas that answer the question, why am I building a Prosperous Home?

Pick one word you wrote that best describes your Purpose and write it here:

____

VISION

In the space below, brainstorm dreams and ideas answering the question, what do I see for my Prosperous Home?

Although you will only have one purpose for your home, you might have multiple visions. For now though, pick one word you wrote that best describes your Vision and write it here: ____________________

STRATEGY

In the space below, list some ways on how you will achieve a Prosperous Home?

Always try to simplify your ideas to one word to help bring clarity and help you remember your answers. Write your Strategies here: ____________________

____________________ ____________________ ____________________

TACTICS

Now that you have brought purpose to your Prosperous Home, which Tactical decisions might you need to add, change, or prioritize?

____________________ (1st priority) ____________________ (4th priority)

____________________ (2nd priority) ____________________ (5th priority)

____________________ (3rd priority) ____________________ (6th priority)

PROSPEROUS HOME

CHAPTER THREE

BALANCE SHEET DISCOVERY

Pg. 47

Your **Assets** Today (at current value):

Cash on Hand	________	Investments	________
Emergency Fund	________	Land	________
Savings	________	Rentals	________
Retirement	________	Intellectual Property	________
Vehicles	________	Other	________
Home	________	Other	________

Total all the assets here: ____________

Your **Debts** Today (at today's balances):

Credit Card #1	________	Home Mortgage	________
Credit Card #2	________	Home Equity Loans	________
Credit Card #3	________	Lines of Credit	________
Car Loan #1	________	Investment Margin Loans	________
Car Loan #2	________	Other Loans	________
Boats & RV Loans	________		

Total all the debts here: ____________

Net Worth: Using the totals above, calculate your net worth using the accounting equation:

+ Total Assets ____________
- Total Debts ____________
=Net Worth ____________

PROSPEROUSHOME
© Stephen K. De Silva ◆ www.prosperoussoul.com

CHAPTER FOUR

TARGET BALANCE SHEET

Pg. 58

	TODAY'S BALANCE SHEET	TARGET AFTER 1 YEAR	CHANGES BY LINE
Cash on Hand			
Emergency Cash			
Savings for a New Car			
Car #1			
Car #2			
Jewelry			
Furniture & Antiques			
Home			
IRA Retirement Savings			
401k Retirement Savings			
TOTAL ASSETS			
Credit Card #1			
Credit Card #2			
Credit Card #3			
Car Loan #1			
Car Loan #2			
Home Mortgage			
TOTAL DEBTS			
NET WORTH			

PROSPEROUSHOME
© Stephen K. De Silva ◆ www.prosperoussoul.com

CHAPTER FIVE

ACTIVE, PASSIVE, & VALUE

INCOME WORKSHEET

Pg. 71

Active Income Streams:

Job #1 Gross Wages (before taxes)	____________
Job #2 Gross Wages (before taxes)	____________
Job #3 Gross Wages (before taxes)	____________
Small Business #1 (net after expenses)	____________
Small Business #2 (net after expenses)	____________
Small Business #3 (net after expenses)	____________
Winning and Prizes	____________

Passive Income Streams:

Interest Income #1	____________
Interest Income #2	____________
Dividend Income #1	____________
Dividend Income #2	____________
Rental Income #1	____________
Rental Income #2	____________
Royalty Income #1	____________
Royalty Income #2	____________

Net Value Changes: ____________

TOTAL INCOME ____________

PROSPER">PROSPEROUSHOME
© Stephen K. De Silva ◆ www.prosperoussoul.com

CHAPTER SIX

LIVING, GIVING, SAVING (LGS) WORKSHEET

Pg. 86

	CURRENT ($)	CURRENT (%)
LIVING		
GIVING		
SAVING		
TOTAL		

	YEAR 1 TARGET ($)	YEAR 1 TARGET (%)
LIVING		
GIVING		
SAVING		
TOTAL		

	DREAM ($)	DREAM (%)
LIVING		
GIVING		
SAVING		
TOTAL		

PROSPEROUS HOME

CHAPTER SEVEN

LGS ANSWER KEY

Pg. 102

If a person has monthly income of:	And an LGS of:	Calculate the:	
$1,000	90/10/0	Monthly Savings:	*$0*
$4,123	80/10/10	Monthly Living:	*$3,298*
$2,444	93/3/4	Monthly Giving:	*$73*
$9,999	70/15/15	Annual Saving:	*$17,998*
$1,901,000	10/57/33	Semi-annual Living:	*$1,140,600*
$1000	90/10/0	Annual Giving:	*$0*

If a person's income is $4,000, and she gives $500 and saves $600, what is she likely spending on living? *$2,900 (4000-500-600)*

If a person is living on $3,000, giving $600, and saving $500, but added new debt of $200, what is her income? *$3,900 (3000+600+500-200)*

If a person is living on 83%, giving 13% and saving 6%, but adds new debt of 2%, what is her saving percentage? *4% (6% - 2%)*

If a person's giving is 13%, how much is his offering percentage? *13% (G=S)*

If a person is living on 102%, how much is his saving percentage? *-2% (100%-102%)*

If a person is living on 100%, how much is his seed? *0% (100% - 100%)*

If a person's combined giving and saving percentage is 30%, how much is his living percentage? *70% (100% - 30%)*

If a person's tithe equals $300, how much is his total income? *$3,000 (300 / 10%)*

PROSPEROUSHOME

CHAPTER EIGHT

LGS MASTER SHEET

Pg. 116-119

	Current	%	Yr 1 Target	%	Yr 2 Target	%	Yr 3 Target	%
INCOME								
Wages & Tips-net								
Interest & Dividends								
Child Support & Alimony								
Gifts/Honoraria Received								
Known Bonus								
Transfer From Savings								
Retirement								
Other								
Other								
TOTAL								
LIVING- HOUSING EXPENSES								
Mortgage/Rent*								
Home/Rental Insurance								
Electricity/Gas/Oil								
Water/Sewer/Trash								
Phone								
Cable/Satellite								
Internet								
Furnishings & Appliances								
Lawn & Garden								
Maintenance & Supplies								
Improvements								
Other								
TOTAL								

PROSPEROUSHOME
© Stephen K. De Silva ◆ www.prosperoussoul.com

CHAPTER EIGHT

(CONTINUED)

	Current	%	Yr 1 Target	%	Yr 2 Target	%	Yr 3 Target	%
LIVING- AUTO EXPENSES								
Car Payments*								
Fuel								
Bus/Taxi/Train Fare								
Repairs								
Registration/License								
Auto Insurance								
TOTAL								
LIVING- PERSONAL EXPENSES								
Groceries								
Dining & Eating Out								
Personal Supplies								
Cleaning, Clothing, & Hair								
Pets								
Other								
TOTAL								
LIVING- HEALTH EXPENSES								
Health Insurance								
Doctor & Dentist								
Medicine & Drugs								
Health Club Dues								
Life Insurance								
Other								
TOTAL								
LIVING- ENTERTAINMENT EXPENSES								
Movies & Music								
Games & Books								
Events & Holidays								
Sports & Hobbies								
Other								
TOTAL								

PROSPEROUSHOME

CHAPTER EIGHT

(CONTINUED)

	Current	%	Yr 1 Target	%	Yr 2 Target	%	Yr 3 Target	%
LIVING- EDUCATION EXPENSE								
Newspaper & Magazines								
Dues & Memberships								
Child Education (All fees)								
Adult Education (All fees)								
Other								
TOTAL								
LIVING- ADMIN & TAX EXPENSE								
Student Loan Minimum*								
Credit Card Minimum*								
Bank Fees & Postage								
Child Support & Alimony								
Taxes								
Other								
TOTAL								
GIVING								
Pledges Paid								
Charitable Donations								
Offerings and Gifts								
Tithe								
TOTAL								
SAVINGS								
Emergency Fund								
Transfer to Savings								
Retirement (401k, IRA)								
Investments								
Education								
Vacation/Travel								
Other								
TOTAL								

PROSPEROUSHOME
© Stephen K. De Silva ◆ www.prosperoussoul.com

CHAPTER EIGHT
(CONTINUED)

	Current	%	Yr 1 Target	%	Yr 2 Target	%	Yr 3 Target	%
DEBT**								
Home Mortgage								
Auto Loan								
Student Loan								
Credit Card Debt								
Other								
TOTAL								
TOTAL INCOME								
TOTAL LIVING								
TOTAL GIVING								
TOTAL SAVING								
TOTAL DEBT								
TOTAL EXPENSES								
SHORTFALL/SURPLUS								

PROSPER
OUSHOME

© Stephen K. De Silva ◆ www.prosperoussoul.com

CHAPTER NINE

OFFERING READING #1

Pg. 132

As we receive today's offering,
We are believing the Lord for:

Jobs and better jobs
Raises and bonuses
Benefits
Sales and commissions
Favorable settlements
Estates and inheritances

Interests and income
Rebates and returns
Checks in the mail
Gifts and surprises
Finding money
Debts paid off
Expenses decrease
Blessing and increase

Thank You, Lord,
for meeting all of my financial needs
that I may have more than enough
to give into the Kingdom of God
and promote the Gospel of
Jesus Christ.

Hallelujah!!!

(See other examples at https://www.ibethel.org/offering-readings/)

PROSPEROUSHOME

CHAPTER TEN

PRIORITY WAR

Pg. 147

Rank from most to least important. List more than three but no more than 10. Create your lists separately first, then present them and engineer the blend. Draw a horizontal line between the priorities where your money runs short.

Husband List	Wife List	Blended List
1.		
2.		
3.		
4.		
5.		
6.		
7.		
8.		
9.		
10.		

PROSPEROUSHOME

© Stephen K. De Silva ◆ www.prosperoussoul.com

CHAPTER ELEVEN

LIFE BRIDGE BALANCE SHEET

Pg. 160

	10 YEARS	50 YEARS	200 YEARS	500 YEARS
Cash on Hand				
Emergency Cash				
Savings for a New Car				
Car #1				
Car #2				
Jewelry				
Furniture & Antiques				
Home				
IRA Retirement Savings				
401k Retirement Savings				
TOTAL ASSETS				
Credit Card #1				
Credit Card #2				
Credit Card #3				
Car Loan #1				
Car Loan #2				
Home Mortgage				
TOTAL DEBTS				
NET WORTH				

PROSPEROUSHOME

CHAPTER TWELVE

LEGACY SPREADSHEET

Pg. 172-174

	AGE:	AGE:	AGE:	AGE:	AGE:	AGE:	AGE:
LIVING							
GIVING							
SAVING							
TOTAL							

	AGE:	AGE:	AGE:	AGE:	AGE:	AGE:	AGE:
LIVING							
GIVING							
SAVING							
TOTAL							

	AGE:	AGE:	AGE:	AGE:	AGE:	AGE:	AGE:
LIVING							
GIVING							
SAVING							
TOTAL							

CHAPTER TWELVE
(CONTINUED)

	AGE:	AGE:	AGE:	AGE:	AGE:	AGE:	AGE:
LIVING							
GIVING							
SAVING							
TOTAL							

	AGE:	AGE:	AGE:	AGE:	AGE:	AGE:	AGE:
LIVING							
GIVING							
SAVING							
TOTAL							

	AGE:	AGE:	AGE:	AGE:	AGE:	AGE:	AGE:
LIVING							
GIVING							
SAVING							
TOTAL							

PROSPEROUSHOME

CHAPTER THIRTEEN

WEALTH MAP

Pg. 194-195

ADOPTION [IDENTITY]

Rom. 8:15 …you have received a spirit of adoption as sons…

God made us significant when we accepted His salvation.

HERITAGE [YOUR TREASURY]

Luke 12:34 For where your treasure is, there your heart will be also.

Peace
Good Name
Integrity
Home Order
Honor
Confidence
Sound Sleep
Friendships

WISDOM [YOUR GARDEN]

Philippians 4:8 Finally, brethren, whatever is true, honorable, right, pure, lovely…

Health
Experience
Education
Training
Talents/Abilities
Alliances
Prophetic Words
Dreams/Passions
Social Skills
Scripture Library
Security
Traditions
Diligence
Perseverance
Focus & Intention
Sabbath
Legacy
Generosity

CHAPTER THIRTEEN
(CONTINUED)

SERVICE [YOUR PLATFORM]
Mark 16:15 And He said to them, "Go…."

City/Region (Citizenship)
Home (Family Leadership)
Work (Marketplace Leadership)
Church (Body of Christ)
Missions (World Leadership)
Government (Political Leadership)
Boardsmanship (Organizational Leadership)

MONEY [YOUR ASSETS]
Matthew 6:33 …and all these things will be added to you.

DooDads
Cash/Equivalents
Certificates Deposit
Treasuries
Stocks/Bonds
Land
Improvements
Home Equity
Life Insurance CSV
Annuities
Commercial Paper/Trust Deeds
Mineral Rights
Intellectual Property
Collectibles
Metals/Gems
Commodities
Ventures And Capital
Currencies

PROSPEROUSHOME

CHAPTER FOURTEEN

DEBT TERMINATOR

Pg. 207

Lender or Bank	Current Balance	Interest Rate(%)	Interest Charges	Minimum Payment	Extra Payment	Balance After
	+		+	-	-	=

ABOUT THE **AUTHOR**

Stephen K. De Silva began his career in 1985 as a certified public accountant. As a self-employed professional, he joined Bethel Church in 1995 to serve as chief financial officer and a member of the senior leadership team. Now Stephen has transitioned to create and teach full-time on subjects related to "money and the prosperous soul." With a unique blend of experience, humor, and anointing, Stephen offers the body of Christ, both domestically and internationally, a fresh, Holy-Spirit–inspired outlook with his biblically based educational insights. The Prosperous Soul family of ministries is based in Redding, California, where Stephen enjoys life with his wife, Dawna, founder and co-leader of the international healing and deliverance ministry Bethel Sozo International.